POSH

TARTS

POSH
TARTS

Over 70 recipes,
from gorgeous galettes to perfect pastries

Pip Spence

Photography by Faith Mason

Hardie Grant

QUADRILLE

Publishing Director: Sarah Lavelle
Editor: Harriet Webster
Series Designer: Gemma Hayden
Designer: Maeve Bargman
Food Stylist and Recipe Writer: Pip Spence
Photographer: Faith Mason
Prop Stylist: Alexander Breeze
Production Controller: Sinead Hering
Production Director: Vincent Smith

Published in 2019 by Quadrille, an imprint of Hardie Grant Publishing

Quadrille
52–54 Southwark Street
London SE1 1UN
quadrille.com

Cataloguing in Publication Data: a catalogue record for this book is available from the British Library.

ISBN 978 178713 381 5

Printed in China

All temperatures given are for fan ovens

CONTENTS

POSH TARTS

★

INTRODUCTION

If someone were to ask me, 'Would you like a slice of this tart I've made?' as well as saying, 'YES please!' I would acknowledge that they've probably gone to a bit of effort to produce this crumbly-pastried, custard-filled, chocolate-studded, tender-fruit-filled, icing-sugar-dusted creation before I've even seen what they've actually baked. That's the thing about making a good tart: however simple or complicated, it does take a degree of skill.

When thinking about tarts my mind tends to wander to pâtisseries in France, from Parisian pastry boutiques full of precision placing and colourful mirror glazes (customers salivating, pastry forks at the ready!), to the rural bakers championing local fruits, nuts and every other regional ingredient available to produce seasonal wonders that would look at home on any country kitchen table. Wherever they are made, all such pastries involve skill and a bit of patience. Some can be patched up if they go wrong – and that's part of the rustic charm – whereas other more intricate recipes need full concentration and a bit of practice to master.

While France may be world-renowned for its pastries, in this book we'll include tarts from all over the world. As well as the obvious sweet treats, we're also covering savoury dishes including quiches, free-form galettes and upside-down onion and butternut squash creations.

Every style and occasion is covered: breakfast and brunch, canapés and starters, midweek meals, dinner party show-stoppers and simple to more complex desserts. Some recipes are suitable for gluten-free, lactose-free and vegan diets, or can be easily adapted.

★

PASTRY BASICS

TYPES OF PASTRY

We can't discuss tarts and not look at pastry. Here are a few of the basics…

Shortcrust pastry and sweet shortcrust pastry (or pâte sucrée) are standard terms but these pastries come in many different forms. The type of fat, flour, flavour, sugar, nuts, eggs and milk used can change the texture, mouthfeel and flavour and can be adapted to complement your chosen filling. Shortcrust takes its name from its texture – 'short' refers to the crumbly nature of the pastry due to its fat content (half fat to flour). It's very sturdy and holds up well.

Puff pastry (shop-bought in this book's case) adds buttery, flaky layers and is the perfect carrier for many sweet and savoury fillings, from apples to crayfish!

Filo pastry is so versatile and its crunchy texture and ease of handling makes it the go-to for quicker bakes.

To save even more time, you can also use shop-bought, pre-baked or pre-made chilled pastry cases. They vary in quality, but some are very good and are useful to have in the cupboard just in case you receive unexpected visitors. In some cases, you don't even need to use pastry at all for tarts or similar dishes. You can use blitzed-up biscuit crumb, baked granola crust, polenta, Parma ham, bread dough and bread slices to line a tart case, and can even bake a quiche without a base.

HINTS & TIPS

Celsius temperatures (°C) are given for fan ovens.

Blind baking pastry (see page 10) means pre-cooking the pastry case before adding the filling. This prevents the pastry from either rising or going soggy, both of which would ruin all your efforts. As you'll see in the book, it's not just shortcrust pastry that benefits from a pre-bake.

Tips for making and using shortcrust pastry...

When making all types of pastry it's really important not to overwork it as this will result in a tough bake. When making shortcrust pastry, rub the butter into the flour using your fingertips to make some large fingernail-size pieces as well as smaller crumbs (as learnt from world-renowned baker Richard Bertinet). I've found using a free-standing bowl mixer with the whisk attachment at this stage stops the mixture from warming up. If you don't have a free-standing mixer, then just make sure your hands are cold as you prepare the pastry – run them under cold water every so often if you feel the mix is becoming too sticky.

Don't add too much liquid to your shortcrust mix. One egg yolk and 1–2 tablespoons of ice-cold water is often enough. Too much liquid results in tough pastry that will shrink, and you'll often find yourself adding extra flour which upsets the whole recipe.

Once you've rubbed the butter into the flour and added any liquid, use a dinner knife to mix everything to a rough dough, then use your hands to bring the mixture together and pat it into a disc. This will make rolling out much easier.

Roll your shortcrust pastry out between two sheets of greaseproof paper. This stops you over-flouring and drying out the pastry. It also makes it much easier to move the pastry around and so achieve an even roll.

Use a wooden spoon handle to push the pastry into the indents of fluted tins. This stops the pastry warming up and helps it keep its shape.

Keep the pastry chilled until you are ready to use it; if your pastry is getting soft just pop it back in the fridge for 10 minutes or so. Don't be tempted to skip the chilling time.

When placing the rolled-out pastry in the tart tin make sure it overhangs the edges. Once blind baked, use a Swiss peeler to trim and tidy up the edges.

Tips for using filo pastry...

When using filo pastry it's important not to let it dry out before you've baked it. It will go brittle and crack. As you work layering up your filo pastry, make sure you brush it well with melted butter or oil, and keep a clean damp tea towel over the remaining pastry to prevent it from drying out.

If you have any raw filo pastry left, roll it up and wrap well in clingfilm (plastic wrap) before storing in the fridge to prevent further drying.

Filo pastry blind bakes really well – the pre-baking helps keep that delicious crisp filo texture throughout. When blind baking it doesn't need as long in the oven as shortcrust.

Filo tarts are best eaten pretty much straight from the oven in my opinion, but you can reheat your tart the following day in a hot oven.

Tips for using puff pastry...

Like shortcrust, puff pastry doesn't respond well to over-working with lots of rolling.

Again use the sheets of greaseproof paper trick to roll out puff pastry and make sure the pastry is well chilled before you start.

You can make life even easier for yourself by buying a sheet or round of ready-rolled sheet puff pastry – perfect for a quick midweek dinner or tarte tatin.

I haven't included a recipe for puff pastry here as it takes at least a day to make and needs photos to explain the technique. There are plenty of baking bibles and online tutorials that can show you this if you would like to make your own.

How to line a tart tin with shortcrust pastry and blind bake...

This is a quick guide to show you the basic principles of lining a tart tin and preparing it for blind baking. This procedure is used a lot in the book so refer back to these pages – it makes

sense not to repeat it over and over. Tart tins come in different shapes and sizes so you need to make sure you have enough pastry to line your tin with enough for some overhang.

If you're making tartlets just cut off enough pastry from the disc and roll one at a time.

Once you've made the pastry, pat it into a disc, cover it in clingfilm (plastic wrap) and leave to rest in the fridge for about 30 minutes, or as specified in the recipe. Unwrap the pastry and place it on a sheet of greaseproof paper that is big enough to allow you to roll out to the desired size and a bit more. Place the same-sized sheet of greaseproof paper on top of the pastry. If the pastry is very hard, use a rolling pin (holding it as if you are about to start rolling) to lightly bash the pastry from top to bottom. Turn it 90 degrees and repeat. Turn a further 90 degrees and repeat once more. This stops you from putting too much pressure on the pastry as you roll, which can cause the pastry to crack.
Now you can start to roll. Roll a few times and continue turning 90 degrees and rolling, then repeat. This ensures the pastry is evenly rolled and doesn't suffer from overworking.

If you have a large sheet of pastry to work with and you feel it's getting too warm you can pick up the whole thing, greaseproof paper and all, and place it back in the fridge for 10 minutes.

Once you've rolled out your pastry to the desired thickness and size, carefully peel off the top layer of greaseproof paper. If the pastry starts to tear then replace the top layer of paper and pop it all back in the fridge. Once you've removed the top layer of paper turn the pastry over and drape it into the tart tin. Carefully peel off the remaining layer of paper then gently ease the pastry into the tin. Holding the overhanging pastry in one hand, work around the tin, gently pressing the pastry into the base and up the sides.

If you're using a fluted tin, once evenly lined, take the handle of a wooden spoon and use it to press the pastry into the indents of the tin. If you are using a non-fluted tin you can use your fingers and thumbs to quickly press the pastry into the tin, but you still want to keep an overhang. Use a fork to prick the base of the pastry all over. Place the case on a baking sheet and put it into the fridge or freezer to chill for at least 30 minutes.

Once the pastry has chilled, remove the case on its baking sheet from the fridge. Preheat the oven (usually to about 180°C/350°F/gas mark 4) and line the case with a piece of greaseproof paper that completely covers the case (you can use a piece from earlier rolling). Fill the lined case to the top with ceramic baking beans, dried rice, beans or lentils. Push the beans well up the sides. Doing this weighs down the pastry to stop air bubbles forming and thus prevents the pastry from rising. It will also help the tart case keep its shape.

Place the case in the oven for between 10 and 20 minutes depending on the size of the tin and the type of shortcrust pastry used. Remove from the oven, spoon out the baking beans and remove the greaseproof paper, then return the case to the oven for a further 5–15 minutes until lightly golden or totally dried out. Return to the oven for a few minutes if it still looks soft.

You can now cool the case, and as it cools in the tin use a Swiss peeler to carefully shave the overhanging pastry away to give a perfectly even-edged tart case.

The case is now ready to be filled.

You can also blind bake puff pastry! Who'd have thought it? It takes around the same time as shortcrust and looks a little rustic but works beautifully for fish-based or fruity bakes, giving flaky pastry with no sogginess!

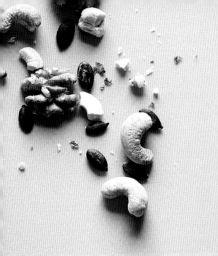

BREAKFAST

TARTS

CHEAT'S

★

PASTÉIS DE NATA

Hailing from the Belém district of Lisbon these tarts are the ultimate sweet treat. Rich and smooth, they are inspired by Rebecca Seal's delicious recipe.

 MAKES 24

TAKES 1 hour 10 minutes, plus cooling time for custard

125g (4½oz) caster (superfine) sugar
300ml (10fl oz) whole milk
1 tsp vanilla bean paste
1 cinnamon stick
3 strips of orange or lemon peel
6 egg yolks
30g (1oz) unsalted butter, melted
2 x 320-g (11-oz) packs pre-rolled all-butter puff pastry
ground cinnamon, plus extra to serve
icing (confectioners') sugar, to serve

First, make the custard. Place the sugar and 5 tbsp water in a small saucepan and bring to the boil. Use a sugar thermometer to check the temperature. Once 105°C (220°F) is reached remove the pan from the heat and place to one side.

Put the milk, vanilla bean paste, cinnamon stick and citrus peel into a medium saucepan and place over a low heat until just bubbling (do not boil). Remove from the heat and place to one side to cool slightly.

Put the egg yolks into a large bowl and whisk well until smooth and thickened. Remove the cinnamon and citrus peel from the milk then very gradually add the milk to the yolks, whisking the whole time.

Pour the custard mix back into the milk pan then add the sugar syrup, whisking as you go. Place the custard pan over the lowest heat, stirring with a spatula continuously, making sure you scrape all the edges to stop the custard from sticking. You want the custard to reach the consistency of double cream, which can take up to 10 minutes.

method continued overleaf...

★ ★ ★ ★ ★ ★ ★ ★ ★ ★ ★ ★ ★ ★ ★ ★ ★

PASTÉIS DE NATA

continued...

Don't let the mixture go above 85°C (185°F) as this may scramble it. As soon as the custard is ready, tip it into a bowl and allow to cool completely. You can cover the custard and place it in the fridge to use the next day. When the custard is cooled preheat the oven to 260°C/480°F/gas mark 9. Lightly grease two 12-hole tart tins with the melted butter.

Unroll one sheet of puff pastry onto a piece of greaseproof paper. Lightly dust the pastry with cinnamon then roll it up into a tight roll. Trim the ends then cut the roll into 12 even rounds. Place a round in the base of one of the tart tin holes so that the swirls are facing upwards, then use your thumbs to work the pastry up the sides of the hole and over the edges a little. You may need to wet your fingers to do this. Repeat with the remaining swirls then spoon 2–3 tbsp custard into each case. Repeat with the second sheet of pastry.

Carefully place the trays in the middle of the oven and bake for about 10 minutes. The custard will spill out, bubble and burn a little but that's perfectly normal. Hopefully the custard will start to caramelise on top, but that doesn't always happen. Remove the tarts from the oven, skirt a knife around each tart to release it from any baked-on custard and allow to cool in the tins for a few minutes before transferring to a wire rack. Serve warm or cold with a dusting of icing sugar and ground cinnamon; they are best eaten the same day. If you have any left store them in an airtight container in a cool place then simply refresh in the oven at 180°C/350°F/gas mark 4 for 5 minutes.

MINI BREAKFAST

★

FRITTATAS

A simple breakfast recipe using three different fillings:
crispy filo with cherry tomatoes and Cheddar, Parma ham
and spinach and herby mushroom.

EACH RECIPE
MAKES 12 mini frittatas
using a 12-hole muffin tin

TOMATO & CHEDDAR
TAKES 40 minutes

PARMA HAM
TAKES 30 minutes

HERBY MUSHROOM
TAKES 40 minutes

TOMATO & CHEDDAR

270-g (9-oz) pack filo pastry
1 tbsp olive oil, plus extra for
    greasing
1 tsp dried oregano
120g (4oz) cherry tomatoes, halved
6 eggs
50ml (2fl oz) milk
a pinch of chilli flakes
70g (2½oz) mature Cheddar
    cheese, grated
sea salt and freshly ground
    black pepper

Preheat the oven to 200°C/400°F/gas mark 6.
Lightly grease the holes of the muffin tin with
olive oil. Cut the filo sheets into 36 squares
approximately 14 x 14cm (5½ x 5½in) to allow a little
overhang. Place one square in each muffin hole
making sure it's carefully pushed down and goes
up the sides. Lightly brush each square with olive
oil and sprinkle with oregano. Place another square
on top at an angle, brush with oil, sprinkle with
oregano and repeat once more. Bake the cases for
10 minutes or until lightly golden. Meanwhile, place
the cherry tomatoes on a roasting tray, season with
salt and pepper and a little olive oil and roast until
the pastry cases are cooked.

Remove the muffin tin from the oven and turn the
oven down to 160°C/325°F/gas mark 3. Crack the
eggs into a bowl and whisk well with the milk and
chilli flakes. Whisk in most of the grated Cheddar,
reserving a little for the tops. Divide the mixture
between the filo cases and gently add the cooked
tomatoes. Top each tart with the remaining cheese.

ingredients and method continued overleaf...

★ ★

MINI BREAKFAST FRITTATAS
continued...

Bake for about 20 minutes until golden and set. If the tarts are a little soft, carefully remove from the tin and place on a baking sheet, then return to the oven for 2 minutes to crisp further.

PARMA HAM

olive oil for greasing
12 slices Parma ham
6 eggs
50ml (2fl oz) milk
75g (2½oz) spinach, chopped
4 spring onions (scallions),
    trimmed and sliced
50g (1¾oz) feta cheese
freshly ground black pepper

Preheat the oven to 160°C/325°F/gas mark 3. Lightly grease the muffin tin and lay a slice of Parma ham into each hole – you may need to trim and stretch them to fit. Crack the eggs into a bowl and whisk well with the milk and a good few grindings of black pepper, then stir in the spinach and spring onions. Divide the mixture between the holes and crumble a little feta into each. Place the tin in the oven and cook for about 20 minutes until golden and set.

HERBY MUSHROOM

1 tbsp olive oil, plus extra for
    greasing
1 tbsp unsalted butter
2 garlic cloves, crushed
200g (7oz) chestnut mushrooms,
    thinly sliced
a few sprigs of thyme, leaves
    picked
a small bunch of flat-leaf parsley,
    leaves chopped
6 eggs
50ml (2fl oz) milk
sea salt and freshly ground
    black pepper

Preheat the oven to 160°C/325°F/gas mark 3. Lightly grease the holes of the muffin tin with a little olive oil. Place a large frying pan over a medium heat and add the olive oil and butter. Once the butter is bubbling add the garlic, mushrooms, thyme and parsley and season well with salt and pepper. In a bowl whisk the eggs with the milk and season well again. Once the mushrooms are cooked, tip onto a plate, allow to cool a little, then mix into the eggs.

Divide the mixture between the holes of the muffin tin. Bake for about 20 minutes until golden and set. Carefully remove the frittatas from the tin by easing a rounded knife around the edge.

FILO

★

BREAKFAST TART

The marriage of a cooked breakfast with crisp and buttery filo pastry is a very good one. Baked eggs are a weekend favourite and pre-baked filo makes the perfect crispy vehicle for them.

 SERVES 4

 TAKES 45 minutes

30g (1oz) unsalted butter, melted
four 37 x 30-cm (14½ x 12-in) filo
   pastry sheets
a few sprigs of thyme, leaves
   picked
120g (4oz) cherry tomatoes
olive oil
3 tbsp Greek yogurt
4 slices (about 100g/3½oz)
   smoked salmon or 6 slices
   cooked, chopped smoked
   streaky bacon
50g (1¾oz) fresh spinach leaves
4 large eggs
10g (¼oz) dill, leaves picked
a few chives, finely chopped
sea salt and freshly ground
   black pepper

Preheat the oven to 200°C/400°F/gas mark 6.

Brush a thin layer of butter all over the base and sides of a 23-cm (9-in) loose-bottom tart tin. Lay over one piece of filo pastry, letting it drape over the edges. Brush butter over this piece and scatter over some thyme leaves. Repeat 3 more times. Gather and crumple up the edges to make a crust and brush this with more butter. Put the tin on a baking sheet and bake for about 10 minutes until lightly golden.

Meanwhile, halve the tomatoes and place in a small roasting tray, drizzle with olive oil and season. Roast for 10 minutes until just cooked.

Turn up the oven to 220°C/425°F/gas mark 7. Spoon the yogurt over the base of the tart case. Arrange the salmon on top of the yogurt then scatter in the tomatoes and spinach leaves, creating 4 indents. Crack the eggs into the indents and season with pepper. Cover loosely with foil and return to the oven for 25 minutes or until the eggs are cooked but the yolks are still runny.

Remove from the oven and scatter over the dill and chives. Serve hot!

ROASTED FRUIT &

★

GRANOLA TARTLETS

Adapt the granola and roasted fruit mixes using whatever you fancy but make sure to use enough oats to achieve the right texture. You can bake the cases the day before and keep them in an airtight container.

MAKES 6

TAKES 35 minutes

140g (5oz) rolled oats
1 tsp ground cinnamon
1 tsp vanilla bean paste
1 tsp ground ginger
40g (1½oz) mixed unsalted nuts, such as almonds, hazelnuts, pecans
20g (¾oz) mixed seeds, such as pumpkin, sunflower, sesame
20g (¾oz) coconut flakes
1 tbsp coconut oil, plus extra for greasing
3 dates, de-stoned
2 tbsp date syrup or maple syrup

For the roasted fruit mix
400g (14oz) mixed fruit, such as apricots, plums, figs, peaches halved, quartered and de-stoned
maple syrup
a sprinkling of ground cinnamon
150g (5oz) soya or natural yogurt, or quark, to serve

Preheat the oven to 180°C/350°F/gas mark 4.

Place the oats, cinnamon, vanilla bean paste, ground ginger, nuts, seeds and coconut flakes in a food processor and blitz to a breadcrumb consistency. Melt the coconut oil in a small saucepan and add to the food processor with the dates and date syrup. Add 2 tbsp cold water then blitz again to form a soft dough.

Place all the fruit into a small roasting tray with a drizzle of maple syrup and the ground cinnamon and roast for about 20 minutes until the fruit is soft and a little caramelised.

Meanwhile, lightly grease 6 mini loose-bottom (10-cm/4-in) tart tins with coconut oil. Divide the oat mixture between the tins and use damp fingers to press the mixture into the bases and up the sides to create tart cases. Place the tins on a baking sheet and bake in the oven for 12–15 minutes until golden. Remove from the oven and allow to cool a little before carefully removing the granola cases from the tins and transferring to a wire rack to cool completely. Serve each case filled with roasted fruit, a spoonful of yogurt and an extra sprinkle of ground cinnamon.

SWEET PEPPER & EGG
★
FOCACCIA

Bread makes a great quick tart case. I've chosen to use
a round focaccia here as it's easy to hollow out and
the herby olive oil bread works brilliantly with all
sorts of fillings.

SERVES 4–6

TAKES 1 hour 15 minutes

1 tbsp olive oil, plus extra for
  drizzling
2 medium onions, peeled and
  thinly sliced
1 large red (bell) pepper, deseeded
  and thinly sliced
2 tbsp tomato purée
2 garlic cloves, crushed
1 tsp sweet smoked paprika
½ x 680g (24oz) jar passata
a splash of balsamic vinegar
1 x 23-cm (9-in) round focaccia
4 eggs
a few sprigs of flat-leaf parsley,
  leaves picked and chopped
a pinch of chilli flakes
sea salt and freshly ground
  black pepper

Heat the oil in a large frying pan over a medium
heat, then add the onions and sauté for 5 minutes.
Add the pepper and cook for a further 5 minutes,
then add the tomato purée, garlic and smoked
paprika and cook, partially covered with a lid, for
10–15 minutes until softened. Add the passata and
bring to the boil. Season with salt and pepper and
add a splash of balsamic vinegar. Reduce the heat
and simmer for 5 minutes until slightly thickened.

Preheat the oven to 200°C/400°F/gas mark 6. Mark
out a 2-cm (1-in) border around the edge of the
focaccia then remove the bread from the centre,
leaving a base. Put the bread from the centre (broken
into small pieces) into a roasting tray, toss with olive
oil and bake for 15 minutes to make croutons.

Place the focaccia onto a baking sheet, drizzle
with a little olive oil and bake for 5 minutes. Spoon
the vegetables into the hollow, create 4 indents
and crack an egg into each one. Loosely cover the
focaccia with an oiled piece of foil and bake for
15–20 minutes, ensuring the yolks are still runny.
Remove from the oven, scatter over the parsley
and sprinkle with chilli flakes. Pop in the middle of
the table, serve with the croutons, slice and eat!

SPRING VEGETABLE ★

BRUNCH TART

Sweet, crunchy veg, smooth ricotta and crisp prosciutto –
a perfect combo! Leave the pastry sheet out of the fridge
for 5 minutes before unfolding so that it doesn't crack.

 SERVES 4

 TAKES 50 minutes

4 small hen's eggs
320-g (11-oz) pack pre-rolled puff
   pastry
150g (5oz) ricotta
20g (¾oz) Parmesan, grated
zest and juice of ½ lemon
50g (1¾oz) fresh peas
100g (3½oz) asparagus spears,
   woody stems removed
4 spring onions (scallions),
   trimmed
1 baby gem lettuce, cut into
   wedges
olive oil
6 slices prosciutto
sea salt and freshly ground
   black pepper

Soft-boil 3 of the eggs for 5–7 minutes. Run under
a cold tap and peel. Place to one side until later.

Preheat the oven to 220°C/425°F/gas mark 7. Place
the pastry on a baking sheet lined with greaseproof
paper. Score a 2-cm (1-in) border around the edge
of the pastry and a criss-cross pattern in the centre.
Be careful not to go through the pastry. Beat the
remaining egg in a mug and brush over the pastry.
Bake for 10 minutes then reduce the temperature
to 160°C/325°F/gas mark 3. Gently push down the
centre of the pastry with the back of a spoon. In a
bowl, mix the ricotta with the Parmesan and lemon
zest and juice then dot this over the centre of the
pastry and bake for a further 15 minutes.

Preheat a chargrill pan over a high heat. Boil the
peas for 2 minutes then drain. Drizzle the asparagus,
spring onions and lettuce with a little olive oil and
griddle in batches until everything is nicely charred.
Place to one side. Turn down the heat and griddle
the prosciutto for a minute on each side until crisp.

Spoon the peas over the ricotta and arrange the
vegetables and prosciutto over the base. Halve
the eggs and nestle them among the vegetables.
Season and serve the tart drizzled with olive oil.

NO-BAKE GREEK YOGURT &
BERRY TART

This lovely little no-bake tart makes a perfect breakfast as it contains no refined sugar. You can prepare the base the night before and chill it in the fridge, then simply top with yogurt and fruit in the morning.

SERVES 6–8

TAKES 20 minutes, plus chilling

2 tbsp coconut oil
100g (3½oz) gluten-free rolled oats
1 tbsp cocoa powder
1 tsp instant coffee powder (not granules)
150g (5oz) mixed nuts and seeds (I've used pecans, poppy seeds, whole almonds and cashews)
a pinch of salt
10 medjool dates, de-stoned
finely grated zest and juice of 1 orange
250g (9oz) Greek yogurt
250g (9oz) frozen mixed berries or frozen mango and pineapple chunks

Melt the coconut oil in a small saucepan over a gentle heat and use a little to lightly grease a 23-cm (9-in) loose-bottom tart tin, then line the base with greaseproof paper (put the remaining oil to one side). Place the oats, cocoa, coffee, nuts and seeds in a food processor with a pinch of salt. Pulse, then add the dates, the remaining coconut oil and the orange juice and pulse again to make a rough dough.

Place the dough in the tart tin and press it over the base and up the sides with the back of a spoon. Trim off any excess and place in the fridge to firm up for at least 30 minutes or overnight.

When ready to serve, carefully remove the case from the tin. (If you have one, use a blowtorch to quickly warm the outside of the tin to soften the coconut oil a little, or pop the tin in a hot oven for 30 seconds to help pop the tart out of the case.) Place the tart on a serving board or plate. Spoon the yogurt into the tart case. Top with the frozen berries in a little pile in the centre, allowing them to run to the edges of the tart and the juice to pool as the berries warm up. Sprinkle over the orange zest, cut into wedges and serve with a coffee.

POLENTA, PEAR &
⭐
BLUEBERRY TART

A comforting, warming gluten-free tart that is lovely eaten
hot or cold on a chilly morning. Try thinly sliced apples
instead of pears if you like.

SERVES 6–8

TAKES 50 minutes

25g (¾oz) unsalted butter, plus
extra for greasing
650ml (23fl oz) milk, almond milk
or hazelnut milk
150g (5oz) quick-cook polenta
sea salt
a small grating of whole nutmeg
2 tbsp runny honey, plus extra for
serving
50g (1¾oz) ground almonds
50g (1¾oz) walnuts
50g (1¾oz) whole hazelnuts
3 pears, cored and thinly sliced
150g (5oz) blueberries
a sprig of rosemary, leaves picked
natural yogurt or fromage frais,
to serve

Preheat the oven to 180°C/350°F/gas mark 4.

Grease and line a baking sheet with greaseproof
paper. In a large saucepan, gently bring the milk to
the boil. Tip in the polenta and whisk well. Add a
pinch of salt and the nutmeg. Continue cooking
and whisking for about 5 minutes until the polenta
is smooth and thickened. Whisk in the honey,
butter and ground almonds then pour the polenta
onto the sheet, spreading it into a 20 x 30-cm
(8 x 12-in) rectangle. Place the sheet in the oven and
bake for about 30 minutes until lightly golden.

Meanwhile, place the walnuts and hazelnuts in a
roasting tray and bake for 10 minutes until golden.
Lightly crush them, then place to one side.

Increase the temperature of the oven to
200°C/400°F/gas mark 6. Once the polenta is baked
remove it from the oven and arrange the sliced
pears over the base. Scatter over the blueberries,
brush over a little honey and sprinkle over the
rosemary leaves. Return the tart to the oven and
bake for 10 minutes or until the fruit has softened
and the pears have started to turn golden. Remove
from the oven and scatter over the roasted nuts.
Serve with natural yogurt or fromage frais.

MEAT

TARTS

QUICHE

LORRAINE

This is a classic French picnic staple and it's always best made from scratch. This version is enhanced with a little kick of wholegrain mustard and fresh rosemary. Serve warm or cold with a peppery salad on the side.

 SERVES 8

 TAKES 1 hour 20 minutes, plus 1 hour chilling

90g (3oz) cold butter, cut into cubes
175g (6oz) plain (all-purpose) flour
1 egg yolk, plus 2 eggs
1 tsp white wine vinegar
200g (7oz) unsmoked bacon lardons
1 tbsp olive oil
1 medium onion, peeled and finely chopped
a sprig of rosemary, leaves picked
120g (4oz) Gruyère or Comté cheese, grated
250ml (9fl oz) double (heavy) cream
2 tsp wholegrain mustard
sea salt and freshly ground black pepper

In a mixing bowl rub the butter into the flour with a pinch of salt and pepper. Stir in 2 tbsp ice-cold water, the single egg yolk and vinegar to make a rough dough. Wrap it in clingfilm (plastic wrap) and chill for 30 minutes.

Fry the lardons for 5 minutes until just golden. Once cooked, tip into a bowl lined with kitchen paper.

Once the pastry has chilled, roll it out to 5mm (¼in) thick and use to line a 20-cm (8-in) fluted loose-bottom tin. Prick the base of the pastry case and chill in the fridge for a further 30 minutes.

Preheat the oven to 180°C/350°F/gas mark 4. Wipe out the frying pan and place it over a low heat. Add the olive oil, followed by the onion and rosemary and fry for 10 minutes until soft and golden.

Blind bake the pastry for 10 minutes then remove the greaseproof paper and baking beans and bake for a further 10 minutes. Allow the case to cool a little then trim the edges. Spoon the lardons and onion into the tart case then scatter over the cheese. Whisk together the 2 eggs, cream, mustard and a pinch of salt and pepper then pour over the filling. Bake for 25 minutes until golden and just set.

SPICED LAMB &
★
AUBERGINE TART

This one takes a little bit of work but is such a delicious
weekend lunch. Lightly spiced, it's full of rich, caramelised
lamb and charred vegetables, a nod to Turkish kebabs.
Serve with pickled chillies to cut through the richness.

 SERVES 4

 TAKES 1 hour 15 minutes

1 large aubergine (eggplant)
2 onions, peeled
1 red (bell) pepper
olive oil
500g (1lb 2oz) (ground) lamb
    mince
2 tsp ground cumin
½ tsp ground cinnamon
2 garlic cloves, crushed
2 tbsp tomato purée
1 large tomato, deseeded and
    chopped
three 37 x 30-cm (14.5 x 12-in)
    filo pastry sheets
1 tsp dried mint
1 lemon
2 tbsp pine nuts, toasted
4 tbsp pomegranate seeds
½ tsp sumac
a bunch of picked flat-leaf parsley
    and mint leaves
sea salt and freshly ground
    black pepper

Preheat the oven to 250°C/475°F/gas mark 9 (or as
high as it will go).

Pop the aubergine, onions and pepper in a small
roasting tray, drizzle over a little olive oil and
season with salt. Place the tray in the oven and
roast for about 35 minutes or until everything is
blackened and soft.

Meanwhile, place a large frying pan over a medium
heat. Add a drizzle of olive oil and crumble in the
lamb. Add the cumin and cinnamon and season
with salt and pepper. Sauté for about 10 minutes
until golden, breaking the meat up well with a
wooden spoon. Stir in the garlic, tomato purée
and tomato. Turn the heat down to low and
partially cover with a lid. Cook, stirring occasionally,
for 20 minutes until golden and quite dry in texture.

Reduce the oven temperature to 200°C/400°F/gas
mark 6.

method continued overleaf...

★ ★ ★ ★ ★ ★ ★ ★ ★ ★ ★ ★ ★ ★ ★ ★ ★

★ ★

TAGINE FILO TART

continued...

1 tsp smoked paprika
a handful of prunes
four 37 x 30-cm (14.5 x 12-in) filo
    pastry sheets
2 tbsp rose harissa
1 x 400-g (14-oz) can chickpeas
    (garbanzo beans)
40g (1½oz) flaked almonds
sea salt

Place the couscous in a heatproof bowl, season
with salt and pepper and add the orange zest, bay
leaves and the smoked paprika. Pour over enough
boiling water to cover the couscous by 1cm (½in).
Place a plate on top and leave for 10 minutes then
fluff the couscous up with a fork.

Remove the tagine from the oven and give it a stir.
Then add the prunes, cover and return to the oven
for a further 1–1½ hours. Once cooked, the meat
should be falling apart and the sauce shouldn't
be too watery; if it is, pop it back in the oven for
5 minutes uncovered. Allow the tagine to cool then
place in the fridge overnight to let the flavours
develop. The next day, take the tagine out of the
fridge 15 minutes before you want to start cooking.

Preheat the oven to 220°C/425°F/gas mark 7. Line a
25-cm (10-in) ovenproof non-stick frying pan with a
sheet of filo pastry. Brush with olive oil and harissa
and place another sheet at an angle on top, then
repeat 2 more times.

Remove the bay leaves from the couscous, spoon it
into the bottom of the pastry case and pat down.
Spoon over the tagine then peel and slice the
orange and arrange this on top. Drain the chickpeas,
pat dry with kitchen paper and toss them with the
remaining paprika, some salt and olive oil. Scatter
the chickpeas and almonds on top of the tart. Fold
the overhanging pastry around the filling to make
a crust, then brush this with the remaining harissa.
Bake the tart for 20 minutes until the pastry is
golden and the filling is piping hot.

WILD MUSHROOM &
★
BACON SLAB

A lovely midweek meal full of slow-cooked sweet leeks,
earthy fried mushrooms, thin-sliced potatoes, salty bacon
and topped with soft and tangy goat's cheese.

 SERVES 4–6

TAKES 55 minutes

20g (¾oz) unsalted butter
3 large leeks, washed and thinly
    sliced
a few sprigs of thyme, leaves
    picked
320-g (11-oz) pack pre-rolled
    all-butter puff pastry
1 egg, beaten
5 slices maple-smoked bacon,
    sliced
250g (9oz) mixed wild mushrooms,
    brushed clean and torn into
    pieces
100ml (3½fl oz) cider or beer
1 tsp Worcestershire sauce
2 new potatoes
olive oil
40g (1½oz) soft goat's cheese
a few sprigs of flat-leaf parsley,
    leaves picked
sea salt and freshly ground
    black pepper

Preheat the oven to 220°C/425°F/gas mark 7. Melt
the butter in a large frying pan over a low heat. Add
the leeks and thyme, stir, then partially cover with a
lid. Cook for 10 minutes until the leeks are soft and
golden, then tip into a bowl.

Unroll the pastry and place on a baking sheet lined
with greaseproof paper. Use a dinner knife to score
a 1-cm (½-in) border around the edge of the pastry
and gently criss-cross in the rectangle in the centre,
taking care not to go through the pastry. Score
slanting lines on the border. Brush the beaten egg
over the pastry and place in the oven for 10 minutes.

Fry the bacon over a medium heat for 5 minutes
until lightly golden, then stir in the mushrooms. Turn
up the heat and add the cider and Worcestershire
sauce. Sauté until the cider has reduced by two-
thirds. Place a lid on the pan and turn the heat down
low. Using a peeler, slice the potatoes into wafer-thin
slices and toss with a little olive oil, salt and pepper.

Remove the pastry from the oven and reduce the
temperature to 180°C/350°F/gas mark 4. Scatter
the leeks, mushroom and bacon mix, potatoes and
goat's cheese over the base. Bake for 10–15 minutes
until golden and crisp. Remove from the oven,
scatter over the parsley and serve.

SAGE, APPLE & SAUSAGE
★
PUFF PIZZA

Who doesn't love a sausage roll?! This tart is basically an open version chock full of all the flavours that go so well with pork... apple, onion, sage and chestnuts.

 SERVES 8

TAKES 45 minutes

500-g (1lb 2-oz) pack puff pastry
plain (all-purpose) flour, for
    dusting
450g (1lb) good-quality sausage
    meat
a small grating of whole nutmeg
1 small onion, peeled and grated
1 small apple, grated
50g (1¾oz) dried apricots, chopped
70g (2½oz) peeled chestnuts
    (canned or vac-packed), roughly
    chopped
a few sprigs of sage, leaves picked
1 egg, beaten
1 tsp sesame seeds
olive oil, for drizzling
sea salt and freshly ground
    black pepper

Preheat the oven to 200°C/400°F/gas mark 6. Line a baking sheet with greaseproof paper.

Roll out the pastry to about 5mm (¼in) thick on a sheet of greaseproof paper and use a large bowl or cake tin as a guide to cut out a 30-cm (12-in) round. Score a 5-mm (¼-in) border around the edge, lightly score a criss-cross pattern in the middle (taking care not to go through the base) and place to one side.

Tip the sausage meat into a large bowl and season well with salt, pepper and nutmeg. Add the onion, apple, apricots and chestnuts. Finely chop most of the sage leaves and add to the sausage meat mixture and mix well.

Spread the mixture over the base of the tart, roughing the mixture up with a fork for texture. Brush the pastry border with the beaten egg and sprinkle over the sesame seeds. Drizzle the remaining sage leaves with a little oil and lay on top.

Place the tart on the lowest shelf of the oven and bake for 30 minutes until golden and risen. Serve with steamed greens or a salad.

CHICKEN, SWEETCORN &

★

ASPARAGUS QUICHE

Sometimes you don't have time to deal with pastry, or you just don't fancy making it. Try this crustless quiche, which is really simple and can be made in less than 30 minutes.

SERVES 4

TAKES 25 minutes

6 large eggs
4 tbsp single (pouring) cream
6 spring onions (scallions), trimmed and sliced
100g (3½oz) asparagus spears, trimmed and thinly sliced, tips left whole
160g (5½oz) shredded smoked chicken breast
100g (3½oz) canned sweetcorn, drained
2 tbsp olive oil
40g (1½oz) rocket (arugula) leaves
balsamic vinegar
sea salt and freshly ground black pepper

Preheat the oven to 200°C/400°F/gas mark 6. Place a 24-cm (9½-in) ceramic flan dish on a baking sheet and place in the oven to heat up.

Meanwhile, crack the eggs into a large mixing bowl and whisk with the cream. Season well with salt and pepper. Stir in the spring onions, asparagus, chicken and sweetcorn.

Remove the flan dish from the oven, pour in the olive oil and swirl it around the dish to coat the base and sides. Carefully tip in the filling and place the quiche back in the oven. Bake for 15–20 minutes until golden and just set.

Remove from the oven and serve warm with balsamic-dressed rocket leaves or a homemade tomato sauce.

ROAST BEEF & RED ONION
★
TARTE TATIN

Red onions work so beautifully when slow-cooked with sugar, red wine vinegar and beef stock. They transform into a rich tarte tatin-style carrier for roast beef and blue cheese. A great way of using up Sunday roast leftovers.

 SERVES 4

 TAKES 1 hour 20 minutes

50g (1¾oz) unsalted butter
3 medium red onions, peeled and
  each cut into 8 wedges
6 garlic cloves, peeled
4 bay leaves
2 tbsp soft light brown sugar
2 tbsp red wine vinegar
1 beef stock cube
a splash of Worcestershire sauce
500g (1lb 2oz) pack puff pastry
50g (1¾oz) blue cheese
50ml (2fl oz) buttermilk
100ml (3½fl oz) soured cream
1 tbsp creamed horseradish
2 tbsp olive oil
200g (7oz) beef fillet (or leftover
  steak or slow-cooked beef)
2 tbsp walnuts, toasted
50g (1¾oz) watercress
a small bunch of chives, chopped
sea salt and freshly ground
  black pepper

Preheat the oven to 200°C/400°F/gas mark 6. Melt the butter in a 24-cm (9½-in) non-stick, ovenproof frying pan over a medium heat. Arrange the red onions in the pan and scatter over the garlic, bay leaves, sugar and vinegar. Crumble in the beef stock cube, add the Worcestershire sauce and season with salt and pepper. Allow to cook on the hob for 5 minutes before covering tightly with foil and placing in the oven for 30 minutes.

Roll out the pastry to 5mm (¼in) thick and cut out a circle 2cm (1in) larger than your frying pan. After 30 minutes remove the pan from the oven and cover the onions with the pastry circle, tucking it all round the edges to form a crisp border. Prick a small hole in the centre to let out any steam. Bake for 35 minutes or until the pastry is puffed up and golden.

Blitz the blue cheese, buttermilk, soured cream, creamed horseradish and 1 tbsp olive oil in a food processor then scrape into a bowl.

Season the beef fillet well with salt and pepper, rub all over with olive oil, then fry to your liking. Flip out the tart onto a serving plate. Slice the beef and arrange on top. Drizzle over a little dressing and scatter over the walnuts, watercress and chives.

CHICKEN WALDORF
⭐
SALAD TARTLETS

Here the classic Waldorf salad is turned into lovely
little mouthfuls on a crouton base. Perfect as
a starter or with drinks.

 MAKES 24

 TAKES 35 minutes

12 slices white bread
20g (¾oz) unsalted butter, melted
1 garlic clove, crushed
200g (7oz) roast chicken, skin
  removed and shredded
50g (1¾oz) free-range egg
  mayonnaise
1 tbsp Dijon mustard
a few sprigs of tarragon, leaves
  picked and chopped
60g (2¼oz) toasted walnuts,
  crumbled
100g (3½oz) natural yogurt
100g (3½oz) green and red seedless
  grapes, cut into quarters
2 celery sticks, thinly sliced at
  an angle
½ small green apple, cored and
  sliced into matchsticks
a few sprigs of chervil, leaves
  picked
sea salt and freshly ground
  black pepper

Preheat the oven to 180°C/350°F/gas mark 4. Roll
out each piece of bread with a rolling pin as thinly
as you can. In a small bowl, mix together the butter
and garlic. Use a 7-cm (2¾-in) round cutter to cut
24 circles from the bread and brush each circle with
the garlic butter.

Press 12 bread circles into the holes of a 12-hole
tart tin. Pop another 12-hole tart tin on top and
place a heavy roasting tray on top of this. Bake
for 10 minutes, then remove the top tart tin and
roasting tray and bake the cases for a further
10 minutes until golden. Remove from the oven and
allow to cool for a few minutes before carefully
removing the cases from the tin and transferring
to a wire rack to cool completely. Repeat with the
remaining bread circles.

Meanwhile, place the chicken in a mixing bowl
and combine with the mayonnaise, mustard and
most of the tarragon and walnuts. Season well with
salt and pepper then fold in the yogurt, grapes,
celery and apple.

Once all the cases are cooked and cooled, fill them
with a spoonful of Waldorf salad and top with a
little sprinkling of walnuts, tarragon and chervil.

QUICHE

I've taken my favourite tapas ingredients and combined them in a quiche with herby flaky pastry. I'm sure I'd get into trouble in Spain for mixing them together but I think they're delicious combined, and I hope you agree!

SERVES 6

TAKES 1 hour 30 minutes, plus 1 hour chilling

125g (4½oz) wholemeal (wholewheat) flour
125g (4½oz) plain (all-purpose) flour
½ tsp fine sea salt
½ tsp smoked sweet paprika
20g (¾oz) grated Parmesan
125g (4½oz) cold butter, cubed
1 egg yolk, plus 4 eggs
50ml (2fl oz) ice-cold water
140g (5oz) soft cooking chorizo
1 medium onion, peeled and finely chopped
100g (3½oz) jarred roasted red peppers, drained
75g (2½oz) frozen peas
150g (5oz) boiled new potatoes, cooled (optional)
150ml (5fl oz) double (heavy) cream
75g (2½oz) Manchego cheese, grated
sea salt and freshly ground black pepper

Start by making the pastry. Place the flours and salt in a large bowl and mix in the smoked paprika and grated cheese. Add the butter and rub it into the flour to lumps the size of your fingernails. Make a well in the centre, add the egg yolk and water, mix in with a dinner knife and then bring everything together into a rough dough with your hands. Tip it out onto a lightly floured work surface, pat into a disc, wrap in clingfilm (plastic wrap) and chill in the fridge for at least 30 minutes.

Place a frying pan over a medium heat. Crumble in the chorizo and fry for a few minutes until the oils are released. Add the onion, turn down the heat and continue to fry for 10 minutes until the onion is golden and softened and the chorizo is a little crispy but still soft. Remove from the heat and place in a large mixing bowl. Tear in the peppers, add the peas and crumble in the potatoes.

method continued overleaf…

CHILLI BEEF TORTILLAS
continued...

To make the tomato salsa, on a large chopping board chop 3 of the tomatoes into medium dice, slice a few stalks of coriander and 2 of the spring onions. Chop to your desired consistency and tip into a serving bowl. Add a squeeze of lime juice and season with salt and pepper.

For the guacamole, on the same board, halve, de-stone and scoop out the avocados. Roughly chop with the remaining tomato, spring onions, a few coriander stalks and pinch of coriander leaves. Spoon into a serving bowl. Add a squeeze of lime juice and season with salt and pepper.

Place the tortilla cups onto a baking sheet, spoon in the chilli and sprinkle each cup with a little more cheese. Return the tarts to the oven for 5 minutes until heated through and the cheese has melted.

Remove from the oven and transfer to serving plates. Top each tart with a spoon of salsa or guacamole and sprinkle over a little remaining coriander and sliced chilli.

ANTIPASTI-TOPPED
★
BAKED POLENTA

Polenta makes such a great base when baked and works
especially well when combined with lots of cheese!
Using quick-cook polenta ensures you won't spend
hours making this tart.

 SERVES 4

 TAKES 45 minutes

olive oil, for greasing
800ml (28fl oz) vegetable stock
170g (6oz) quick-cook polenta
50g (1¾oz) unsalted butter
50g (1¾oz) Parmesan cheese,
   grated
150g (5oz) chestnut mushrooms,
   halved
a splash of white wine vinegar
100g (3½oz) ricotta
50g (1¾oz) jarred smoked
   tomatoes (or semi-dried),
   drained
10 slices bresaola
10 slices thin-cut salami
50g (1¾oz) jarred grilled artichoke
   pieces, drained
a small handful of black olives,
   pitted
sea salt and freshly ground
   black pepper

Preheat the oven to 200°C/400°F/gas mark 6.
Grease a deep 25-cm (10-in) loose-bottom tart tin
with olive oil, line the base with greaseproof paper
and place to one side.

In a large saucepan bring the vegetable stock to
the boil, turn the heat down to medium and pour
in the polenta, whisking continuously. Turn the
heat down to low and cook for 3 minutes until the
polenta is thick and blipping. Once cooked, stir in
half the butter and the Parmesan then season well
with salt and pepper. Pour the polenta into the tin,
allow it to settle a little, then use a spoon to even
out the base and push the polenta up the edges of
the tin. Make an indent in the centre. Put the tart
case on a baking sheet and bake for 25 minutes or
until set and a little crisp.

Meanwhile, melt the remaining butter in a frying
pan over a medium heat. Add the mushrooms and
sauté for 5 minutes. Add the vinegar, season with
salt and pepper and place to one side.

Once the polenta base is cooked allow it to cool
completely then arrange the mushrooms and
remaining antipasti on top.

SEAFOOD

★

TARTS

HADDOCK, PRAWN &
SPINACH FILO TARTS

A light starter that can be made into one large tart using a 25-cm (10-in) tart tin. You can swap the smoked haddock for salmon fillet if you fancy; the poaching time will be the same. Serve with a green salad and lemon wedges.

 SERVES 12 (as a starter)

TAKES 45 minutes

2 bay leaves
500ml (17½fl oz) milk
7 black peppercorns
1 small onion, peeled and halved
200g (7oz) smoked haddock fillets, skin on and pin boned
1 garlic clove, crushed
55g (2oz) unsalted butter
60g (2¼oz) baby leaf spinach
20g (¾oz) plain (all-purpose) flour
50g (1¾oz) Cheddar cheese
75g (2½oz) raw, shelled king prawns (jumbo shrimp), cut in half
four 40 x 30-cm (16 x 12-in) filo pastry sheets
3 tbsp olive oil
a few chives, roughly chopped

Place the bay leaves, milk, peppercorns, onion and smoked haddock in a frying pan. Over a medium heat, allow the milk to come up to a slow bubble. Poach the fish for 5 minutes, then turn off the heat and leave the fish to sit in the milk for a few minutes.

Place the garlic in a medium frying pan, add 15g (1 tbsp) of the butter and place over a low heat. Let the butter melt and gently cook for 3 minutes then tip the garlic butter into a small bowl and place to one side.

Pop the spinach into the saucepan, turn up the heat a little and stir the until wilted. Spoon into a clean muslin or dish cloth and squeeze the liquid out of the spinach. Chop up, then tip into a large bowl, stir in the garlic butter and place to one side.

method continued overleaf...

★ ★ ★ ★ ★ ★ ★ ★ ★ ★ ★ ★ ★ ★ ★ ★

★ ★

EASY PISSALADIÈRE
continued...

Preheat the oven to 220°C/420°F/gas mark 7. Lightly oil a 35 x 25-cm (14 x 10-in) baking sheet and sprinkle with the polenta.

Once the dough has risen, knock back and tip onto a lightly floured work surface. Roll into a rough rectangle to fit the baking sheet. Place this 'pizza' base on the prepared baking sheet and use your fingers to stretch the dough to the edges.

Spoon the onion topping evenly over the base, leaving a border around the edge. Brush a little olive oil around the crust. Arrange the anchovy fillets into a lattice pattern on top then pop an olive in the middle of each diamond. Put the pissaladière in the oven and bake for 20 minutes or until the base is golden, turning the sheet halfway. Serve hot.

HOT SMOKED SALMON
★
WATERCRESS QUICHE

A timeless flavour combination that can happily grace any
lunch table. Delicious warm or cold and perfect eaten
any time of year.

 SERVES 6–8

TAKES 1 hour 15 minutes,
plus chilling

500g (1lb 2oz) pack all-butter
   shortcrust pastry
a little plain (all-purpose) flour,
   for dusting
1 tbsp olive oil
1 medium onion, peeled and
   finely chopped
4 eggs
50ml (2fl oz) milk
200ml (7fl oz) double (heavy)
   cream
70g (2½oz) watercress, chopped,
   saving a few sprigs for garnish
150g (5oz) hot smoked salmon
sea salt and freshly ground
   black pepper

Preheat the oven to 180°C/350°F/gas mark 4.

Roll out the pastry to 3mm (⅛in) thick between
2 sheets of greaseproof and use to line a 24-cm
(9½-in) loose-bottom tart tin or quiche dish. Prick
the base with a fork, line the base with greaseproof
paper and chill in the fridge for 30 minutes.

Meanwhile, place a small frying pan over a low heat,
add the olive oil, onion, and a good pinch of salt
and pepper and fry for 10 minutes until just golden.
Tip into a bowl and place to one side.

Remove the pastry case from the fridge, place on
a baking sheet and blind bake in the oven for
15–20 minutes. Remove from the oven, take out
the greaseproof paper and baking beans and bake
for a further 15–20 minutes until lightly golden.

Meanwhile, whisk the eggs in a large bowl with
a good pinch of pepper. Pour in the milk, cream,
onion and most of the watercress and whisk again.
Pour the mixture into the tart case then flake in
chunks of hot smoked salmon. Place the tart in the
oven and bake for 25 minutes until set and golden.

Serve warm or cold with a scattering of watercress.

TONNATO
★
TART

The classic Italian tuna-based tart is addictive.
Most of the ingredients will be found in your store
cupboard but fresh tomatoes top it off really well,
turning sweet as they bake.

SERVES 4

TAKES 1 hour 30 minutes

olive oil, for greasing
30-cm (12-in) pre-rolled puff
   pastry round
220g (7¾oz) good-quality tuna
   in olive oil, drained (150g/5oz
   drained weight)
3 anchovy fillets in olive oil
finely grated zest and juice
   of 1 lemon
2 tsp baby capers
2 tsp Dijon mustard
150g (5oz) crème fraîche
1 egg
50g (1¾oz) Emmental cheese
150g (5oz) mixed heritage
   tomatoes, thinly sliced
olive oil
125g (4½oz) Tenderstem broccoli
125g (4½oz) fine green beans,
   trimmed
freshly ground black pepper

Preheat the oven to 200°C/400°F/gas mark 6. Line a greased 23-cm (9-in) ceramic tart dish with the round of puff pastry, pushing it to the edges and rolling up over the edges to make a crust. Prick the base with a fork and line with greaseproof paper. Fill with baking beans and blind bake for 15 minutes then remove the greaseproof paper and baking beans and bake for a further 10 minutes.

Reduce the oven temperature to 180°C/350°F/gas mark 4. Mix the tuna, anchovy fillets, lemon zest, capers, Dijon mustard, crème fraîche, egg and a good pinch of black pepper in a bowl. Sprinkle the Emmental over the base of the tart and pour in the tuna mix. Arrange the tomatoes over the top, drizzle with olive oil and bake for 30 minutes or until golden. Once the tart is cooked, switch the oven off and leave it to set for 20 minutes.

Meanwhile, trim and boil the broccoli and green beans in a large saucepan for 2 minutes, then drain. Griddle the vegetables over a high heat for a few minutes until charred and just cooked. Tip into a bowl and dress with olive oil and lemon juice.

Remove the tart from the oven and serve warm or cold with the griddled greens on the side.

SMOKED MACKEREL & HORSERADISH
★
OATY TARTLETS

The base of these simple little tartlets is quite similar in taste and texture to an oatcake and works perfectly for strong flavours such as smoked fish or blue cheese.

MAKES 24

TAKES 35 minutes

190g (6¾oz) rolled oats
2 tbsp sesame seeds
2 tbsp pumpkin seeds
1 tsp fennel seeds
50g (1¾oz) unsalted cashews
a sprig of rosemary, leaves picked
2 tbsp soy sauce
2 tbsp olive oil, plus extra for
  greasing
1 tbsp maple syrup
90g (3oz) good-quality cream
  cheese
180g (6¼oz) smoked mackerel
  fillet, skinned
zest and juice of 1 lemon
1 tbsp creamed horseradish
1 punnet salad cress
a few beetroot (beet) crisps or
  1 tsp beetroot (beet) powder
  (optional)
freshly ground black pepper

Preheat the oven to 180°C/350°F/gas mark 4. Lightly grease the holes of two 12-hole mini muffin tins.

Blitz the oats, seeds, cashews, and rosemary in a food processor. Add the soy sauce, olive oil, pepper, maple syrup and 4 tbsp cold water. Blitz again to form a rough dough.

Fill each hole of the muffin tins with the oat mixture, using wet fingers to press it up the sides to form tart cases. Bake the cases for 12 minutes until golden. Remove from the oven, allow to cool a little, then carefully remove the cases from the tins, transfer to a baking sheet and return to the oven to crisp up for 2 minutes. Remove from the oven and pop on a wire rack to cool completely.

Place the cream cheese, mackerel fillets, lemon zest and juice, horseradish and a good pinch of pepper in a bowl and mix well (you can do this in a food processor to make a smoother pâté, if you like). Arrange the cooled cases on a board. Drop a generous teaspoon of the cheese and fish mixture into each case, add a pinch of salad cress to the top of each one and a beetroot crisp or pinch of beetroot powder, if using, then season with a little pepper. Serve straight away.

CRAB

TART SOUFFLÉ

This is a real twist on a classic soufflé and is quite the show-stopper. A perfect starter for a dinner party or when you want to impress (...and actually it's not that tricky!).

 SERVES 8

TAKES 1 hour 20 minutes

500g (1lb 2oz) pack unsweetened shortcrust pastry
50g (1¾oz) plain (all-purpose) flour, plus extra for dusting
50g (1¾oz) unsalted butter
300ml (10fl oz) whole milk
1 tsp English mustard
3 eggs, separated
finely grated zest of 1 lemon
a small bunch of chives, finely chopped
200g (7oz) fresh picked white crabmeat
50g (1¾oz) Gruyère cheese, finely grated
20g (¾oz) Parmesan cheese, finely grated
cayenne pepper
sea salt and freshly ground black pepper

Preheat the oven to 180°C/350°F/gas mark 4. Roll out the pastry to 3mm (⅛in) thick on a lightly floured work surface and use it to line a 23-cm (9-in) loose-bottom tart tin, leaving the pastry to overhang a little. Blind bake in the oven for 15 minutes then remove the greaseproof paper and baking beans and bake for a further 10 minutes until lightly golden. Trim the pastry edges once cool.

Place the flour, butter and milk in a saucepan and stir over a medium heat until thickened and smooth. Allow to cool a little then whisk in the mustard, egg yolks, lemon zest, most of the chives and good pinch of black pepper. Place to one side.

Beat the egg whites to stiff peaks in a clean mixing bowl using an electric hand whisk. Carefully fold these into the sauce mixture and then fold in the crabmeat and cheeses until just incorporated. Spoon the soufflé mixture into the tart case and bake in the oven for about 30 minutes or until golden and risen. Remove from the oven, sprinkle over the remaining chopped chives and a light dusting of cayenne pepper. Serve immediately.

SALMON & BEETROOT IN
★
SOUR PASTRY

Soured cream pastry gives this tart a lovely rustic twist; it's
super flaky and gorgeously crumbly. Earthy beetroots top
a light smoked salmon and potato filling, which is then
encased in a cream cheese sauce.

 SERVES 4–6

 TAKES 2 hours, plus chilling

175g (6oz) plain (all-purpose) flour
150g (5oz) cold unsalted butter,
  cubed
90ml (3fl oz) soured cream
200g (7oz) beetroots (beets),
  scrubbed clean and cut
  into 1-cm (½-in) thick slices
olive oil
2 tbsp pumpkin seeds
150g (5oz) floury potatoes,
  scrubbed and thinly sliced
1 large egg, beaten
150ml (5fl oz) double (heavy)
  cream
100g (3½oz) cream cheese
100g (3½oz) smoked salmon
sea salt and freshly ground
  black pepper

In a bowl rub the butter into the flour with a pinch
of salt. Add the soured cream and bring together to
form a dough. Roll out to 3mm (⅛in) thick and use
to line a 20-cm (8-in) loose-bottom tart tin, allowing
for overhang. Prick the base and chill in the fridge
for 30 minutes.

Preheat the oven to 180°C/350°F/gas mark 4. Toss
the beetroots with olive oil in a small roasting tray
and roast for 20 minutes. Place the pumpkin seeds
in a small dish and toast in the oven for a few
minutes. Place a saucepan of water on to boil with
a pinch of salt. Boil the potato slices for 4 minutes
then drain in a colander. Allow to steam dry.

Blind bake the pastry case for 20 minutes. Remove
the paper and beans, brush with egg and return to
the oven for a further 15 minutes until golden. Mix
the remaining egg, double cream and cream cheese
in a jug and season. Pop a few spoonfuls of sauce
in the base of the pastry case. Layer the potatoes
and smoked salmon, add the remaining sauce and
top with the beetroots. Bake for 30 minutes until
firm. Remove the tart from the tin, place on a baking
sheet and bake for another 10 minutes. Allow to cool
for 10 minutes, then sprinkle with pumpkin seeds.
Serve warm or cold.

CREAMY AVOCADO &
★
CRAYFISH TART

Crayfish are plump and sweet, and go especially well with minty peas and avocado. Fresh and superbly simple to make, this open tart is a great addition to a lunch. Make all the components separately and take along to a picnic.

 SERVES 6–8

 TAKES 30 minutes

33-cm (13-in) round of ready-rolled puff pastry
1 egg, beaten
a pinch of sweet smoked paprika
150g (5oz) frozen peas
4 sprigs of mint, leaves picked
1 lemon
2 ripe avocados
240g (8½oz) cooked crayfish tails
4 spring onions (scallions), white and green ends sliced and separated
a few chives, sliced
3 tbsp Greek yogurt
1 tbsp free-range egg mayonnaise
sea salt and freshly ground black pepper

Preheat the oven to 180°C/350°F/gas mark 4.

Place the puff pastry round on a baking sheet lined with greaseproof paper. Brush the pastry with a little beaten egg and sprinkle with a pinch of salt and sweet smoked paprika. Bake the pastry in the oven for about 20 minutes until golden and risen.

Meanwhile, place the peas in a sieve in the sink and pour over boiling water from the kettle. Tip the peas from the sieve into a food processor. Add half the mint leaves, a good pinch of salt and pepper and a squeeze of lemon juice. Blitz well and tip into a small bowl.

Halve, de-stone and peel the avocados and dice the flesh. Drizzle with a little lemon juice and tip into a bowl followed by the crayfish tails, the white ends of the spring onions, the chives and a good pinch of pepper. Fold in the yogurt and mayonnaise and place to one side.

Once the pastry has cooked remove it from the oven, allow to cool then transfer to a serving board. Push down the centre of the pastry, spoon in the pea mixture then top with the crayfish filling and scatter over the sliced green spring onion.

COQUILLES SAINT JACQUES
★
TARTLETS

This recipe is a take on the classic French dish of fresh scallops in a creamy white wine sauce, cooked in scallop shells and topped with Duchess potatoes.

 SERVES 8

 TAKES 1 hour 25 minutes

200g (7oz) floury potatoes, peeled
30g (1oz) butter, plus a knob for melting
a few gratings of whole nutmeg
1 egg yolk
200ml (7fl oz) fish stock
100ml (3½fl oz) dry white wine
1 x 180-g (6¼-oz) pack small fresh roe-less scallops
100g (3½oz) chestnut mushrooms, quartered
1 lemon
1 banana shallot, peeled and finely chopped
2 tbsp plain (all-purpose) flour
2 tbsp crème fraîche
eight 8-cm (3-in) pre-baked unsweetened shortcrust pastry cases

Chop the potatoes into large chunks and place in a medium saucepan of water with a good pinch of salt. Bring to the boil and cook for about 10 minutes. Drain the potatoes in a colander and allow to steam dry for 1 minute. Return to the pan and place over a low heat. Add 10g (¼oz) of the butter and the nutmeg and mash well. Take off the heat and whisk in the egg yolk with a good pinch of salt and pepper. Take a large piping bag with a large star or plain nozzle, fill with the mashed potato mix and place to one side.

Meanwhile, place the fish stock and wine in a shallow saucepan and simmer over a low heat. Add the scallops and poach them for 1 minute until they have just turned white. Remove the scallops from the pan with a slotted spoon and place in a bowl. Keep the stock to one side.

ingredients and method continued overleaf...

★ ★ ★ ★ ★ ★ ★ ★ ★ ★ ★ ★ ★ ★ ★ ★

★ ★

COQUILLES SAINT JACQUES TARTLETS

continued...

2 tbsp fresh breadcrumbs
a few sprigs of flat-leaf parsley
    or chervil, leaves picked and
    chopped, keeping a few for
    garnish at the end
baby spinach leaves, wilted
sea salt and freshly ground
    black pepper

Place the mushrooms in a medium frying pan with the juice of half the lemon and a good pinch of salt and pepper. Add a splash of water and place the pan over a medium heat for about 10 minutes until the liquid has evaporated. Then tip the mushrooms into the bowl of scallops.

Place the reserved stock in a saucepan over a medium heat and reduce the liquid by about half. Meanwhile, place a small pan over a low heat, add the remaining butter and, once melted, add the shallot. Cook for about 2 minutes, stirring continuously, then stir in the flour and cook for about 1 minute until bubbling. Whisk in the stock and any juice from the scallops and continue to stir and cook for about 3 minutes over a low heat until bubbling and the sauce coats the back of a spoon. Whisk in the crème fraîche.

Preheat the oven to 200°C/400°F/gas mark 6.

Place the pastry cases onto a baking sheet. Mix the scallops and mushrooms into the sauce and spoon into the pastry cases. Take the piping bag of mashed potato and pipe a wreath of potato around the border of each tart. Mix the breadcrumbs and parsley in a bowl with the knob of melted butter and sprinkle over the filling in the centre.

Place the tarts in the oven and bake for 20 minutes until bubbling and golden. Allow to sit for 5 minutes before serving alongside the wilted spinach.

VEGGIE

★

TARTS

TARTE

★

FLAMBÉE

A traditional and light quiche–pizza hybrid, this speciality
of the French Alsace region and southwest Germany
is topped with a thin layer of caramelised onions,
crème fraîche and rosemary.

SERVES 4–6 (2 tarts)

TAKES 1 hour, plus 1 hour
proving

300g (10½oz) strong white bread
  flour, plus extra for dusting
¼ tsp table salt
½ x 7g (¼oz) sachet dried
  fast-action yeast
1 tsp runny honey
olive oil
3 tbsp butter
750g (1lb) onions, peeled and
  thinly sliced
2 garlic cloves, peeled and sliced
a sprig of rosemary, leaves picked
  and chopped
130ml (4½fl oz) crème fraîche
1 egg
50g (1¾oz) Gruyère cheese, grated
½ tsp caraway seeds
a pinch of sweet smoked paprika
sea salt and freshly ground
  black pepper

Place the flour and salt in a bowl and make a well
in the middle. Combine the yeast, honey, a splash
of olive oil and 120ml (4fl oz) lukewarm water. Once
the mixture is frothing, tip it into the well and use a
dinner knife to bring the mixture together. Knead the
dough on a lightly floured surface for a few minutes
until elastic. Lightly oil the bowl, tip the dough back
in and cover with clingfilm (plastic wrap). Put in a
warm place for an hour or until doubled in size.

Meanwhile, melt the butter in a frying pan over a
low heat. Stir in the onions, garlic and rosemary with
a pinch of salt. Sauté for 20 minutes until the onions
are softened then remove from the heat. In a mixing
bowl whisk the crème fraîche and egg with a pinch
of salt and pepper, then stir in the Gruyère.

Preheat the oven to 220°C/430°F/gas mark 7. Knock
back the dough and tip it onto a lightly floured work
surface. Cut in half and roll each ball into a 30-cm
(12-in) long oval. Transfer each one to a lightly floured
baking sheet. Arrange the onions over the bases
then pour the crème fraîche mix over. Sprinkle over
the caraway seeds and smoked paprika. Bake the
tarts for 20 minutes or until the onions have started
to brown and the base is crisp. Serve hot or cold.

PASTRY

Chicory (endive) fry and roast really well, keeping a slight crunch, and partner up beautifully with smooth, strong blue cheese. Combined here with sweet rosemary pecan brittle and buttery pastry base this is deliciously decadent.

 SERVES 4–6

 TAKES 1 hour 15 minutes, plus chilling

100g (3½oz) unsalted butter, cut into 1-cm (½-in) cubes and popped in the freezer for 30 minutes
175g (6oz) plain (all-purpose) flour
sea salt
olive oil
100g (3½oz) caster (superfine) sugar
50g (1¾oz) pecans
3 sprigs of rosemary, leaves picked
3 heads of white and red chicory (endive), halved lengthways
1 orange
1 egg, beaten
100g (5oz) blue cheese (Stilton works well)

To make the pastry, put the frozen butter cubes in a food processor with the flour and a good pinch of sea salt. Pulse a few times to make chunky breadcrumbs. Add 5 tbsp ice-cold water and pulse again to form a very rough dough. Tip out onto a clean work surface and bring the dough together lightly with your hands. Pat into a disc shape, wrap in clingfilm (plastic wrap) and chill in the fridge for 1 hour.

Lightly grease a sheet of greaseproof paper with olive oil and place it on a baking sheet. To make the brittle, place the caster sugar in a non-stick frying pan over a medium heat with a splash of water. Once the sugar has melted allow to bubble for about 5 minutes until the sugar has turned a light chestnut-brown colour. Don't stir the sugar, just swirl the pan a little. As soon as it is brown tip in the pecans, rosemary and add a good pinch of salt. Carefully swirl everything around in the pan to coat and tip onto the greaseproof paper. Allow to cool.

method continued overleaf...

GLUTEN-FREE BROCCOLI & ROMESCO TART

continued...

30g (1oz) pecorino cheese, grated
sea salt and freshly ground
   black pepper

Reduce the oven temperature to 180°C/350°F/ gas mark 4. Once the pastry has chilled, remove it from the fridge and roll out to 3mm (⅛in) thick between 2 pieces of greaseproof paper. Cut a circle big enough to line a 20-cm (8-in) tart tin, allowing a little overhang. Prick the base of the pastry with a fork and chill in the fridge for 30 minutes.

Place a medium saucepan of water on to boil and cook the broccoli florets for 3 minutes. Drain and drop into a bowl of cold water. Drain again and pat dry with kitchen paper. In a large jug whisk together the eggs, cream and pecorino, season well with salt and pepper, then place to one side.

Once the pastry case has chilled, place it on a baking sheet. Blind bake for 20 minutes then remove the greaseproof paper and baking beans and return to the oven for a further 15 minutes until lightly golden. If any cracks appear in the pastry mix a little raw pastry with water and paint over the cracks. Brushing the case with beaten egg and returning to the oven for 2–3 minutes also helps seals the cracks.

When baked, remove the case from the oven, trim the edges with a Swiss peeler, then spoon the romesco sauce over the base. Arrange the broccoli florets on top and then pour over the egg mix. Place the tart back in the oven and bake for about 20 minutes until golden and just set. Serve warm or cold with a green salad.

ACORN SQUASH &
★
CARROT TARTE TATIN

Sweet or savoury? Tasting a little bit like pumpkin pie this
tart works beautifully as a starter or main served with a
peppery salad and a crumbly cheese like Lancashire, or
serve with fresh fruit, crème fraîche and mint as a dessert.

SERVES 4–6

TAKES 1 hour 20 minutes

1 x 500g (1lb 2oz) onion squash
125g (4½oz) carrots, peeled
olive oil
½ tsp ground cinnamon
chilli flakes
33-cm (13-in) round of ready-
   rolled unsweetened shortcrust
   pastry
2 tbsp chestnut purée
a few sprigs of lemon thyme
2 tbsp soft light brown sugar
50g (1¾oz) salted butter
a splash of red wine vinegar
a few gratings of whole nutmeg
sea salt and freshly ground
   black pepper

Preheat the oven to 200°C/400°F/gas mark 6.

Peel, deseed and cut the squash into 3-cm (1¼-in)
wedges. Cut the carrots into 3-cm (1¼-in) rounds.
Toss the vegetables in a roasting tray with 2 tbsp
olive oil, the cinnamon, a good pinch of chilli flakes
and some salt and pepper. Roast for 30 minutes.

Meanwhile, unroll the pastry round onto a sheet of
greaseproof paper. Spread the chestnut purée over
one side of the pastry then place to one side.

Once cooked, transfer the roasted vegetables to
a 24-cm (9½-in) non-stick ovenproof frying pan.
Arrange in 1 or 2 layers, using the carrots to fill in
any gaps. Tuck in the lemon thyme sprigs. Place
the pan over a medium heat then scatter over the
sugar and butter. Increase the heat and allow the
sugar to bubble and become golden. Add a splash
of vinegar and remove from the heat.

Place the pastry over the frying pan, purée side
down, and crimp a little at the edge. Bake the tart
for 20–30 minutes or until golden.

Once baked carefully turn the tart out onto a plate
and sprinkle over the nutmeg. Serve hot or cold.

HERITAGE

★

TOMATO TART

A good-quality pre-made pastry case is a brilliant ingredient to have on standby for surprise guests or when you're pressed for time. Here it's used simply with beautiful heritage tomatoes and creamy, herby goat's cheese.

 SERVES 6

TAKES 10 minutes

200g (7oz) heritage (heirloom) tomatoes
125g (4½oz) soft goat's cheese
150g (5oz) ricotta cheese
a splash of milk
a bunch of chives, chopped
1 tsp finely grated lemon zest
20-cm (8-in) pre-made unsweetened shortcrust pastry case
½ tsp dried oregano
extra virgin olive oil
sea salt and freshly ground black pepper

Slice the larger tomatoes and cut the small ones in half and place to one side. Place the goat's cheese, ricotta and milk in a small bowl and mix until smooth. Add a good pinch of black pepper, most of the chives and the lemon zest and mix again.

Spoon the cheese mixture into the pastry case. Arrange the tomatoes on top then sprinkle with a little oregano, the remaining chives, salt and a drizzle of extra virgin olive oil. Cut into slices and serve.

ROASTED VEGETABLE

★

GALETTE

This is a great Christmas centrepiece, chock full of festive favourites! Earthy mushroom duxelle, sweet roasted carrots, parsnips and squash encased in crisp wholemeal pastry. Serve with potatoes, lots of gravy and greens!

SERVES 6

TAKES 2 hours, plus chilling

450g (1lb) chestnut mushrooms
50g (1¾oz) unsalted butter
3 shallots, peeled and finely chopped
3 tbsp dry white wine
a small bunch of tarragon, leaves picked and chopped
1 tbsp breadcrumbs
200g (7oz) plain (all-purpose) flour
50g (1¾ oz) wholemeal plain (wholewheat all-purpose) flour, plus extra for dusting
150g (5oz) cold unsalted butter, cubed
1 egg yolk, plus 1 egg
1 tsp cider vinegar
2 medium parsnips, peeled
200g (7oz) baby carrots
250g (9oz) butternut squash, peeled
olive oil
2 tbsp runny honey

Place the mushrooms in a food processor and blitz well. Melt the butter in a frying pan over a medium heat then add the mushrooms, shallots and a good pinch of salt and pepper and cook, stirring occasionally, for about 20 minutes or until the liquid has evaporated. Tip in the wine, stir well and cook for a further 5–10 minutes until nearly dry. Mix in the tarragon and breadcrumbs then leave to one side.

To make the pastry, place both the flours in a large mixing bowl with a pinch of salt. Rub the butter into the flour then make a well in the centre and add the egg yolk, vinegar and 2 tbsp ice-cold water. Mix with a dinner knife then bring the dough together with your hands. Pat into a disc, wrap in clingfilm (plastic wrap) and chill in the fridge for 30 minutes.

Preheat the oven to 200°C/400°F/gas mark 6.

ingredients and method continued overleaf...

★ ★ ★ ★ ★ ★ ★ ★ ★ ★ ★ ★ ★ ★ ★ ★ ★

★ ★

ROASTED VEGETABLE GALETTE

continued...

2 tbsp dried cranberries
2 tbsp hazelnuts, lightly bashed
sea salt and freshly ground
    black pepper

Cut the parsnips into batons, the carrots in half and the butternut squash into chunks. Place the vegetables in a roasting tray and toss with 1 tbsp olive oil, salt and pepper. Roast in the oven for about 40 minutes until cooked but not too golden. Halfway through cooking turn the vegetables and drizzle over the honey.

Once the pastry has firmed up, remove from the fridge and roll out between 2 sheets of greaseproof paper into an oblong approximately 25 x 35cm (10 x 14in) in diameter and 3mm (⅛in) thick. Place the pastry onto a baking sheet lined with one of the pieces of greaseproof paper. Spread the mushroom mixture over the oblong, leaving a 1-cm (½-in) border around the edge. Arrange the roasted vegetables over the mushrooms and scatter over the cranberries and hazelnuts. Beat the remaining egg with a fork. Carefully lift the pastry edges up and over the vegetables on the outer sides to form a crust. Brush the crust with beaten egg and place the tart in the oven for 30 minutes until crisp and golden. Serve hot.

pictured opposite: Garden of Veggie Roses, see page 102

GARDEN OF
★
VEGGIE ROSES

This fun, vegan tart needs a little time to roll up the
vegetable roses but it's worth it! A perfect centrepiece,
it's inspired by Barbara at BuonaPappa.net

SERVES 6

TAKES 1 hour 50 minutes

33-cm (13-in) round of ready-
  rolled puff pastry
150g (5oz) vegan soft cheese
1 garlic clove, crushed
50g (1¾oz) ground almonds
2 tbsp fresh breadcrumbs
1 medium yellow courgette
  (zucchini)
2 medium green courgettes
  (zucchini)
1 white or yellow carrot
2 medium orange carrots
2 medium purple carrots

For the pistou
a small bunch of mixed flat-leaf
  parsley and basil (keep a few
  small leaves to garnish)
a few chives
finely grated zest and juice
  of 1 lemon
4 tbsp olive oil
sea salt and freshly ground
  black pepper

Preheat the oven to 180°C/350°F/gas mark 4. Line
a 22-cm (8½-in) loose-bottom tart tin with the
pastry then blind bake for 20 minutes. Meanwhile,
mix together the vegan soft cheese, garlic, ground
almonds, breadcrumbs and a pinch of salt and
pepper in a bowl. Place to one side.

Trim all the vegetables then peel them into long
strips. Microwave the strips for 30 seconds or place
batches of the strips into a colander in the sink and
pour boiling water over them, then allow to drain.

Remove the greaseproof paper and baking beans
from the pastry case then bake for a further
5–10 minutes until golden. Once baked, spoon the
cheese mixture into the base. Tightly roll up one
vegetable strip, surround with a second strip and
roll up around the first piece. Place the vegetable
'rose' in the centre of the tart. Repeat and arrange
the roses all over the tart. Drizzle with olive oil
then bake the tart for 40–50 minutes until golden.

To make the pistou, whizz all the ingredients in a
food processor and pour into a serving bowl.

When the tart is ready, serve hot or cold with a
drizzle of pistou and the reserved herb leaves.

HERITAGE BEETROOT &
★
FETA SLICE

Sweet beetroot and tangy feta cheese set in a light yogurt
'custard' makes a delicious filling for crisp filo pastry
layered with nuts and breadcrumbs.

SERVES 4

TAKES 2 hours

450g (1lb) heritage beetroots
  (beets), scrubbed and cut
  into 3-cm (1¼-in) chunks
olive oil
1 small red onion, peeled and
  sliced into thin rounds
2 tbsp red wine vinegar
1 tsp caster (superfine) sugar
four 40 x 30-cm (16 x 12-in) filo
  pastry sheets
2 tbsp breadcrumbs
70g (2½oz) shelled, unsalted
  pistachios, chopped
1 garlic clove, crushed
100g (3½oz) feta cheese
175g (6oz) Greek yogurt
2 egg yolks
sea salt and freshly ground
  black pepper

Preheat the oven to 200°C/400°F/gas mark 6. Toss
the beetroots in a roasting tray with 2 tbsp olive
oil and season well with salt and pepper. Cover the
tray with foil and roast for 40 minutes.

Toss the onion in a bowl with the vinegar, sugar and
a good pinch of salt. Mix well and leave to pickle.

Grease a 35 x 12-cm (14 x 5-in) loose-bottom tart
tin with olive oil. Lay a sheet of filo pastry in the
tin and brush with oil. Mix the breadcrumbs with
half of the pistachios and scatter a quarter of the
mixture over the filo. Repeat 3 more times so that
you have 4 layers. Bake the case for 15 minutes.

Remove the foil from the beetroots and roast for a
further 20 minutes. In a mixing bowl whisk together
the garlic, feta, yogurt and egg yolks. Season well
with salt and pepper.

When the pastry is baked and beetroots cooked it's
time to assemble. Reduce the oven temperature to
160°C/320°F/gas mark 3. Spoon the yogurt mix over
the pastry, arrange the beetroot on top and bake
for 20 minutes. Scatter over the pickled onions and
remaining pistachios and serve hot.

GARLIC

★

MUSHROOM CUPS

These simple little canapés taste a bit like deep-fried
breaded garlic mushrooms. Very moreish!

🍴 MAKES 24 TARTLETS

⏰ TAKES 15 minutes

2 tbsp unsalted butter
2 garlic cloves, crushed
175g (6oz) mixed wild mushrooms,
   brushed clean and large ones
   torn in half
3 sprigs of thyme, leaves picked
a splash of brandy
1 egg
3 tbsp double (heavy) cream
24 mini canapé cases or Swedish
   croustade cases
3 tbsp red onion marmalade
sea salt and freshly ground
   black pepper

Preheat the oven to 200°C/400°F/gas mark 6.

Melt the butter in a frying pan over a low heat then
add the garlic. Stir in the mushrooms and thyme
and season with a good pinch of salt and pepper.
Turn up the heat and sauté for about 5–10 minutes
until the mushrooms are golden. Add the brandy
and turn up the heat to cook off the alcohol.
Remove from the heat.

In a jug whisk together the egg and cream.

Arrange the canapé or croustade cases on a baking
sheet and spoon a little red onion marmalade into
the base of each one. Top with the mushrooms
and pour over a little of the egg mix (about 2 tsp
in each). Place the tartlets in the oven and bake for
5 minutes. Once warmed through remove from the
oven and serve immediately.

PESTO PASTRY

★

CAULIFLOWER CHEESE

This is a great one to serve as a main for vegetarian guests,
or you can treat it like a fondue if you serve it straight
from the oven; give everyone little cubes of potato,
pickles and ham for dipping into the oozy centre.

 SERVES 6

TAKES 1 hour 40 minutes,
plus chilling

300g (10½oz) plain (all-purpose)
  flour
175g (6oz) cold unsalted butter,
  diced
1 egg yolk, plus 2 eggs
2 tbsp basil pesto
300g (10½oz) cauliflower, cut into
  small florets
olive oil
400ml (14fl oz) whole milk
50g (1¾oz) mature Cheddar
  cheese, grated
30g (1oz) Red Leicester cheese,
  grated
2 tsp wholegrain mustard
2 tbsp Parmesan cheese, grated
4 tbsp fresh breadcrumbs
a few sprigs of thyme, leaves
  picked
sea salt and freshly ground
  black pepper

In a large bowl rub together 250g (9oz) flour with
125g (4½oz) butter and a pinch of salt. Add the
egg yolk, pesto and 1 tbsp ice-cold water. Bring the
pastry together into a rough dough, wrap in clingfilm
(plastic wrap) and chill in the fridge for 30 minutes.

Preheat the oven to 200°C/400°F/gas mark 6. Toss
the cauliflower in a roasting tray with a drizzle of
olive oil and salt and pepper. Roast for 20 minutes.
Meanwhile, melt the remaining butter in a saucepan
over a low heat. Once bubbling, stir in the remaining
flour then whisk in the milk. Cook, gently stirring,
for 5 minutes until thickened. Stir in the cheeses
and the mustard, season, and place to one side.

Roll out the pastry to 3mm (⅛in) thick and use to
line a 23-cm (9-in) quiche dish. Prick the base all over,
trim the edges and chill in the fridge for 30 minutes.
Turn the oven down to 180°C/350°F/gas mark 4.

Blind bake the pastry case for 20 minutes then
remove the greaseproof paper and baking beans and
bake for a further 5–10 minutes until golden. Whisk
the remaining 2 eggs into the cheese sauce then add
the cauliflower. Spoon into the pastry case. Sprinkle
over the Parmesan, breadcrumbs and thyme, drizzle
with olive oil and bake for 25 minutes. Serve warm.

Veggie Tarts

BAKED CAMEMBERT WITH
★
FILO DIPPERS

Is this a tart? Well, it's a cheese wrapped in a pastry case so I'm saying yes! A Christmas classic made into a fun sharing starter, turning extra filo pastry into dippers, and served with roasted grapes, crudités and cranberry sauce.

  SERVES 4

TAKES 30 minutes

1 x 250-g (9-oz) Camembert cheese
1 garlic clove, peeled and sliced
a sprig of rosemary, leaves picked
five 30 x 40-cm (12 x 16-in) filo
 pastry sheets (2 cut in half and
 3 cut into quarters)
50g (1¾oz) unsalted butter, melted
200g (7oz) grapes, cut into small
 bunches
crudités (a mix of carrot, celery
 and cucumber batons)
4 tbsp cranberry sauce

Preheat the oven to 220°C/420°F/gas mark 7.

Score a criss-cross pattern on the top of the cheese and stud with slices of garlic and rosemary leaves.

Lightly grease a 12-cm (5-in) ovenproof dish or loose-bottom tart tin. Lay one sheet of the halved filo sheets over the tart tin and brush with a little butter, layer over another piece at a 45-degree angle, brush with butter and repeat twice more. Place the Camembert in the middle and gather up the pastry around the edges then brush all over with butter. Place on a baking sheet.

Take the remaining quarter sheets of pastry, brush each with a little butter and scrunch into mini parcels. Brush with a little more butter and place on the baking sheet.

Place the grape bunches onto the baking sheet and bake everything for 20 minutes until the pastry is golden and the cheese melted. Serve with the roasted grapes, crudités and cranberry sauce.

SPINACH PESTO, CHEESE &
★
POTATO TART

Like classic cheese and potato pie, simple ingredients speak
for themselves. I've added a delicious pesto to the mix,
too, as it brings an extra freshness to the cheese fest!

 SERVES 6

TAKES 1 hour 45 minutes,
plus chilling

500g (1lb 2oz) pack unsweetened
  shortcrust pastry
3 tbsp Parmesan cheese, grated
25g (¾oz) walnuts, toasted
1 garlic clove, peeled
finely grated zest and juice of
  ½ lemon
100g (3½oz) fresh spinach
olive oil
250g (9oz) baby new potatoes,
  very thinly sliced
100g (3½oz) Taleggio cheese,
  sliced, or mature Cheddar
  cheese, grated
2 eggs
1 tbsp double (heavy) cream
  or crème fraiche
sea salt and freshly ground
  black pepper

Sprinkle 1 tbsp Parmesan over the top of the pastry
then roll out to 3mm (⅛in) thick. Use it to line a
20-cm (8-in) loose-bottom tart tin then trim the
edges and prick the base all over. Chill in the fridge
for 30 minutes.

Meanwhile, make the pesto. Blitz the walnuts,
garlic, lemon zest and juice, spinach and 2 tbsp
olive oil in a food processor. Season with salt and
pepper, stir in the remaining Parmesan and loosen
with more oil if needed. Place to one side. Cook
the potatoes in boiling water for 2 minutes. Drain in
a colander and tip onto a plate lined with kitchen
paper. Pat dry and toss in a little olive oil.

Preheat the oven to 180°C/350°F/gas mark 4.
Remove the pastry case from the fridge, place on a
baking sheet and blind bake for 15 minutes. Remove
the greaseproof paper and baking beans and return
the case to the oven for 10 minutes until golden.

Spoon a third of the pesto into the tart case, add a
layer of potatoes then season well. Top with some
cheese then repeat twice more. Beat together the
eggs and cream and pour over the filling. Cover the
tart with foil and bake for 30 minutes. Remove the
foil and bake for a further 15 minutes until golden.

ROASTED

★

RATATOUILLE TART

Roasted sweet Mediterranean vegetables are the base of this easy bake. Turn it into a vegan dish if you want by using puff pastry made with vegetable oil instead of butter and vegetarian Parmesan for grating.

 SERVES 6

TAKES 55 minutes

1 medium aubergine (egg plant), cut into 2-cm (¾-in) thick rounds
1 medium courgette (zucchini), cut into 2-cm (¾-in) thick rounds
150g (5oz) cherry tomatoes, halved
1 yellow (bell) pepper, deseeded and cut into thin strips
1 medium red onion, peeled and sliced into wedges
3 garlic cloves, skin on and lightly crushed
1 tbsp dried oregano
1 tsp dried mint
3 tbsp olive oil
4 tbsp passata
33-cm (13-in) round of ready-rolled puff pastry
3 tbsp whole milk or almond milk
1 tbsp finely grated Parmesan
sea salt and freshly ground black pepper
a few sprigs of fresh parsley, leaves picked and chopped
a few chervil leaves (optional)

Preheat the oven to 180°C/350°F/gas mark 4.

Place all the vegetables in a large roasting tray and season with most of the dried herbs (reserving a little of each for sprinkling later), olive oil, salt and pepper. Roast for about 30 minutes.

Meanwhile, unroll the pastry onto a baking sheet lined with greaseproof paper. Score a 4-cm (1½-in) border around the edge of the pastry. Score the centre of the pastry and place in the oven for 15 minutes.

Once the vegetables are cooked, remove them from the oven and place to one side. Spoon the passata over the centre of the pre-baked pastry circle. Arrange the vegetables on top and brush the edges with milk. Sprinkle over the remaining dried herbs, half of the grated Parmesan and a good pinch of salt and pepper.

Place the tart in the oven and bake for 15 minutes. Once the tart is baked, remove from the oven, scatter over the remaining Parmesan and fresh herbs and serve warm.

FRUIT

★

TARTS

JAM

★

TARTS

Jam tarts are a standard in the repertoire of any young child growing up in the UK and a great introduction to making pastry for little ones. A small piece of nostalgia.

 MAKES 18 TARTS

TAKES 30 minutes, plus chilling

225g (8oz) plain (all-purpose) flour
25g (¾oz) ground almonds
sea salt
125g (4½oz) cold butter, cubed, plus 20g (¾oz) extra, melted, for greasing
1 egg yolk
125g (4½oz) fruit jam (jelly) or curd

Put the flour, ground almonds and a pinch of salt into a large mixing bowl and rub in the butter. Make a well in the centre and add the egg yolk and 1 tbsp ice-cold water. Bring the dough together using a dinner knife then use your hands to pat it into a disc. Cover in clingfilm (plastic wrap) and chill in the fridge for 30 minutes.

Preheat the oven to 180°C/350°F/gas mark 4.

Lightly grease the holes of two 12-hole shallow tart tins. Take the pastry from the fridge and roll out to about 5mm (¼in) thick. Take a 7-cm (3-in) round or fluted pastry cutter and cut out 18 rounds. You may need to re-roll the pastry to make all 18. Use the leftover pastry to cut out decorations for the top of your tarts. Line the holes of the tart tin with the pastry circles and fill each with 1–2 tsp jam or curd. Put any pastry decorations on top.

Bake the tarts in the oven for about 15 minutes or until the jam bubbles a little. Remove from the oven and transfer to a wire rack. Be sure these have cooled before you eat them otherwise the filling will burn your mouth.

CHRISTMAS STREUSEL

★

TARTS

A lovely Christmas recipe full of warming spices and sweet and sour fruit with a crunchy, crisp traditional German streusel topping. Serve these tarts warm with a dollop of brandy cream.

MAKES 8 TARTS

TAKES 1 hour 15 minutes, plus chilling

200g (7oz) unsalted butter, softened, plus 75g (2½oz) cold unsalted butter, cut into cubes
150g (5oz) golden caster (superfine) sugar
a pinch of table salt
finely grated zest of 1 orange
½ tsp ground cinnamon
2 egg yolks
475g (1lb 1oz) plain (all-purpose) flour
½ tsp baking powder
400g (14oz) good-quality mincemeat
1 cooking apple, cored and coarsely grated
40g (1½oz) dried unsweetened cranberries
icing (confectioners') sugar, to serve

Beat the butter in a large mixing bowl with 100g (3½oz) of the caster sugar and a pinch of salt until light and fluffy. Add the orange zest, cinnamon and egg yolks and briefly mix again. Sift in 350g (12oz) of the flour and fold until just incorporated. Wrap in clingfilm (plastic wrap) and chill in the fridge for 1 hour.

To make the streusel topping, in a mixing bowl rub together the 75g (2½oz) butter with the baking powder and remaining flour and sugar until you have a mix of larger and smaller pieces. Pinch some together to make even bigger pieces. Tip onto a baking sheet and chill in the fridge for 30 minutes.

Once the pastry has chilled roll out to 3mm (⅛in) thick. Cut out eight 12-cm (5-in) pastry circles and use to line eight 10-cm (4-in) fluted loose-bottom tart tins, allowing overhang. Prick the base of each pastry case and chill in the fridge for 30 minutes.

ingredients and method continued overleaf...

★★★★★★★★★★★★★★★★★

DUTCH APPELTAART

continued...

Take the remaining pastry from the fridge and cut off a second third. Roll this out to make two equal-sized strips, each about 30 x 4cm (12 x 1½in), that will line the sides of the tin. Pinch and patch everything together making sure the side panels overlap onto the base piece to prevent leaking.

Preheat the oven to 180°C/350°F/gas mark 4.

Brush the inside of the pastry case all over with beaten egg. Mix the breadcrumbs in with the apples and use to fill the pastry case.

Take the final third of pastry and roll out again to make a round slightly larger than the tart. Cut the pastry into 1cm (½in) strips. Bring the outside edges of the tart slightly over the filling. Lattice the pastry strips over the top of the tart and brush all over with the remaining beaten egg, then sprinkle with a little caster sugar.

Place the tart on a baking sheet and bake in the oven for about 1 hour until bubbling and golden. Remove the tart from the oven and allow to cool for a few minutes in the tin before carefully turning it out onto a serving plate. If the base is a little undercooked simply place the tart on a non-stick heavy baking sheet and pop back into the oven for 10–15 minutes with a piece of foil over the top of the tart to stop it from browning too much. Serve warm with whipped cream.

CHERRY BAKEWELL
★
SLICE

Bakewell tart is a 'modern' version of the Bakewell pudding created in the Derbyshire town of the same name, possibly in the late 1800s. Ready-made shortcrust pastry works well against the sweet frangipane and sour cherry.

 SERVES 8–10

TAKES 1 hour 15 minutes, plus chilling

500g (1lb 2oz) pack shortcrust pastry
160g (5½oz) unsalted butter, softened
160g (5½oz) caster (superfine) sugar
2 medium eggs
160g (5½oz) ground almonds
2 tsp almond extract
100g (3½oz) cherry jam (jelly)
2 tbsp flaked almonds
3 tbsp icing (confectioners') sugar
50g (1¾oz) glacé or fresh cherries, to decorate

Roll out the pastry to about 3mm (⅛in) thick, and use to line a 35 x 12-cm (14 x 5-in) rectangular loose-bottom tart tin, allowing overhang. Prick the base and chill in the fridge for 1 hour.

Meanwhile, make the frangipane. In large bowl mix the butter, caster sugar, eggs, ground almonds and almond extract and place to one side.

Preheat the oven to 180°C/350°F/gas mark 4. Blind bake the pastry case for 15 minutes. Remove the greaseproof paper and baking beans and bake for a further 10 minutes until golden. Allow to cool slightly then trim the edges.

Spoon the jam into the base of the tart then spread over the frangipane and sprinkle over half of the flaked almonds. Bake for 30 minutes until just set then allow to cool for a few minutes before removing from the tin and transferring to a wire rack to cool completely. Toast the remaining almonds in a small pan on the hob for 5 minutes until golden.

Once cooled, mix the icing sugar with enough cold water to make a thick drizzling consistency. Zigzag the icing over the tart, arrange the cherries on top and scatter over the almonds. Cut into slices and eat.

SPANISH-STYLE ORANGE
★
ALMOND TART

Loosely based around the flavours of Torta de Santiago from Galicia, this easy orange tart can be put together in minutes and makes a fantastic addition to a teatime spread.

 SERVES 8

 TAKES 45 minutes

120g (4oz) unsalted butter,
  softened
70g (2½oz) golden caster
  (superfine) sugar
2 eggs
finely grated zest of 1 orange,
  plus a few orange slices for
  decoration
200g (7oz) ground almonds
a splash of Spanish brandy or
  sherry (optional)
20-cm (8-in) ready-made sweet
  shortcrust pastry case
150g (5oz) orange marmalade
18 blanched almonds

Preheat the oven to 180°C/350°F/gas mark 4.

Place the butter and caster sugar in a mixing bowl and beat well until pale and fluffy. Crack in the eggs and beat then fold in the orange zest, ground almonds and brandy or sherry, if using, then place to one side.

Put the pastry case on a baking sheet and spoon 100g (3½oz) of the marmalade over the base, spreading it out in a thin layer. Spoon the almond filling on top of the marmalade and smooth over. Arrange the almonds and a few thin slices of orange on top and bake the tart in the oven for 25–30 minutes until just set.

Remove from the oven and leave to cool in the tin for a few minutes, then carefully remove the tart from the tin and transfer to a wire rack to cool until just warm. Warm the remaining marmalade in a small saucepan then brush this over the tart. Slice and serve.

PINEAPPLE & RUM

★

COCONUT TART

Warming chilli-spiked spiced rum mixed with fresh
pineapple – this is such an easy crowd-pleaser.

SERVES 6–8

TAKES 55 minutes, plus
steeping

4 tbsp spiced rum
1 red chilli, halved and deseeded
1 star anise
1kg (2lb 4oz) pineapple, peeled,
 cored and chopped (you need
 about 600g/1¼lb flesh)
3 eggs
2 tsp cornflour (cornstarch)
70g (2½oz) soft light brown sugar
100g (3½oz) desiccated coconut
20-cm (8-in) pre-baked, sweet
 shortcrust tart case
2 tbsp coconut flakes

Place the rum in a small saucepan with half the
chilli and the star anise. Bring to the boil, simmer
for 2 minutes then turn off the heat. Meanwhile,
place 400g (14oz) of the pineapple in a medium
bowl. Tip the infused rum over the pineapple and
steep for 30 minutes. Drain the pineapple, keeping
the chilli rum, and leave to one side.

Preheat the oven to 180°C/350°F/gas mark 4.

Place the tart case on a baking sheet. Crack the
eggs into a medium bowl with the cornflour
and 50g (1¾oz) soft light brown sugar and whisk
together. Fold in the steeped pineapple and
desiccated coconut. Spoon this filling into the case.
Bake in the oven for 25 minutes until golden and set.

Meanwhile, place a large frying pan over a high
heat. Add the remaining pineapple and fry until
golden, then add the remaining brown sugar and
stir. Add the reserved chilli rum, then carefully light
with a lit match and flambé.

Cool the tart on a wire rack then transfer to a
serving plate. Pile the flambéed pineapple in the
middle. For more spice, finely chop the remaining
half chilli and sprinkle over the tart with the
coconut flakes. Serve warm.

BABY

★

BANOFFEE PIES

This retro 1970s British dessert, that many think is a North American invention, sits firmly in the hearts of many pudding lovers. Banoffee apparently stands for banana and coffee (not toffee as often assumed)!

 SERVES 6

 TAKES 3 hours 25 minutes, plus cooling

180g (6¼oz) digestive biscuits (graham crackers)
2 tbsp walnuts, lightly toasted
1 tsp instant coffee powder
100g (3½oz) salted butter, melted, plus extra for greasing
1 x 397g (14oz) can condensed milk (or 397g ready-made dulce de leche)
½ tsp sea salt
2–3 small/medium bananas
300ml (10fl oz) double (heavy) cream
100g (3½oz) milk chocolate

Take six 10-cm (4-in) loose-bottom tart tins and lightly grease the base and sides of each one. Cut out 6 circles of greaseproof paper and line the base of each.

Place the digestive biscuits, walnuts and coffee in a food processor and blitz to a sandy texture. Tip into a bowl, stir in the melted butter and mix well.

Divide the mixture between the tins. Pat down with a spoon and use your fingers to press the mixture over the bases and up the sides of the tins. Place the pie cases in the fridge to firm up for at least 1 hour.

To make the dulce de leche sauce, place the whole can of condensed milk into a medium saucepan. Fill the pan with cold water, making sure there is at least 5cm (2in) of water covering the can. Place the pan over a high heat and bring to the boil. Reduce the heat to a low simmer and cook the can for 3 hours.

method continued overleaf...

★ ★ ★ ★ ★ ★ ★ ★ ★ ★ ★ ★ ★ ★ ★ ★ ★

★ ★

QUINCE PASTA FROLA

continued...

Once the tart case has chilled, remove from the fridge and place on a baking sheet. Scatter the pine nuts into the base and spoon in the quince jelly, spreading evenly until it comes just under the rim (allowing space for apricots to be added and the jelly to bubble in the oven). Arrange the apricots on top.

Roll out the remaining pastry and cut into roughly 1-cm (½-in) thin strips for the lattice pattern. Beat the remaining egg. Arrange the pastry strips as a lattice on top and brush over the beaten egg to secure the strips and glaze the pastry.

Bake the tart in the oven for 30–40 minutes until golden. While it is baking gently heat the apricot jam in a small pan. Once the tart is cooked, remove from the oven and allow to cool for a few minutes before carefully removing it from the tin and transferring it to a wire rack. Brush the tart with the apricot jam and allow to cool completely. Dust with icing sugar before serving.

PEACH & RASPBERRY
★
GALETTE

A galette or crostata-style tart works for all seasons with so many fruits, no tart tins needed. Peach and raspberry are a lovely summery combo but you can use any berries as well as nectarines, plums, pears, apples…

SERVES 6–8

TAKES 55 minutes, plus chilling

200g (7oz) plain (all-purpose) flour
50g (1¾oz) icing (confectioners') sugar
50g (1¾oz) ground almonds
a pinch of table salt
150g (5oz) chilled unsalted butter, cut into cubes
1 egg, plus 1 egg white
200g (7oz) ripe peaches, halved and de-stoned
50g (1¾oz) raspberries
1 lemon
3 tbsp caster (superfine) sugar
1 tbsp plain (all-purpose) flour
½ tsp ground cinnamon
a few gratings of whole nutmeg
2 tbsp peach or raspberry jam (jelly)
a few sprigs of mint

Mix the flour, icing sugar, ground almonds and a pinch of salt in a mixing bowl. Rub in the butter then make a well in the centre. Crack in the egg with 2 tbsp ice-cold water and use a dinner knife to bring it together into a rough dough. Wrap in clingfilm (plastic wrap) and chill in the fridge for 30 minutes. Preheat the oven to 190°C/375°F/ gas mark 5.

Slice the peaches and place in a bowl with the raspberries. Add a squeeze of lemon juice to the fruit, toss, then sprinkle over 2 tbsp caster sugar, 1 tbsp flour, the cinnamon and nutmeg, then mix.

Roll out the pastry to a rough 30-cm (12-in) circle, 3mm (⅛in) thick. Transfer to a baking sheet lined with greaseproof paper.

In a small bowl mix the jam with a little squeeze of lemon juice. Spread most of the jam over the base of the pastry leaving a 4-cm (1½-in) border. Arrange the fruit over the jam. Fold the pastry border over the fruit then brush the egg white over the border. Brush the fruit with the remaining jam and sprinkle all over with the remaining caster sugar. Bake the galette for 30 minutes until the pastry is golden. Serve hot with vanilla ice cream.

TARTE AU
★
CITRON

Buttery, biscuity pastry and deliciously tart citrus filling –
a delicate French classic.

 SERVES 8

TAKES 1 hour 20 minutes,
plus chilling

260g (9oz) unsalted butter,
softened
180g (6¼oz) caster (superfine)
sugar
4 eggs, plus 6 egg yolks
finely grated zest of 3 lemons
200g (7oz) plain (all-purpose) flour
250ml (9fl oz) lemon juice (freshly
squeezed)
40g (1½oz) candied lemon peel,
to decorate
icing (confectioners') sugar, for
dusting

In a large mixing bowl beat 90g (3oz) of the butter and 60g (2¼oz) of the caster sugar until light and fluffy. Beat in 2 egg yolks one at a time with the zest of 1 lemon. Mix in the flour and bring the dough together with your hands. Wrap in clingfilm (plastic wrap) and chill in the fridge for 30 minutes.

Meanwhile add the lemon juice and remaining zest to a medium saucepan with the remaining butter and caster sugar, the 4 eggs and 4 yolks. Stir continuously over a low heat for 2–3 minutes until the mixture thickens and coats the back of the spoon. Pass through a sieve into a clean bowl.

Roll out the pastry to 3mm (⅛in) thick and use it to line a 20-cm (8-in) loose-bottom tart tin. Prick the base all over and chill in the fridge for 30 minutes. Preheat the oven to 180°C/350°F/gas mark 4.

Blind bake the chilled pastry case for 15 minutes. Remove the greaseproof paper and baking beans and bake for a further 10 minutes. Allow to cool, then trim the edges. Reduce the oven temperature to 160°C/320°F/gas mark 3. Pour the filling into the case and bake for 20 minutes. Allow to cool slightly, then remove from the tin and transfer to a wire rack. Serve cold with, dusted with icing sugar and with the candied lemon peel in the centre.

KEY LIME

★

PIE

The traditional key lime pie is, of course, made using the lovely little Key variety of limes named after the Florida Keys. They are very hard to get hold of outside of Mexico and the Americas, so using regular limes is fine.

 SERVES 12

 TAKES 55 minutes, plus cooling

150g (5oz) sweet crumbly biscuits (like digestives, graham crackers or Hobnobs)
150g (5oz) ginger nut biscuits
3 dates, de-stoned
120g (4oz) unsalted butter, melted, plus extra for greasing
4 egg yolks
595g (1lb 3oz) canned condensed milk (roughly 1½ cans)
finely grated zest and juice of 7 limes (you need roughly 200ml (7fl oz) juice)
300ml (10fl oz) double (heavy) cream
2 tbsp icing (confectioners') sugar
2 limes, to decorate

Preheat the oven to 160°C/320°F/gas mark 3. Lightly grease a 30 x 20-cm (12 x 8-in) rectangular loose-bottom tart tin.

Blitz the biscuits to a fine crumb in a food processor. Add the dates and blitz again. Tip into a large bowl and stir in the melted butter. Mix well then tip the crumbs into the tart in and pack them in well over the base and up the sides. Bake the tart case for 15 minutes, then remove from the oven and allow to cool.

Whisk the egg yolks in a large bowl until pale and thickened. Add the condensed milk and whisk again for a couple of minutes. Whisk in the lime zest and juice for a further 2 minutes. Pour the mixture into the tart case and return to the oven for 15–20 minutes until just set. Remove the tart from the oven, allow to cool slightly, then carefully remove it from the tin and place on a serving plate. Chill in the fridge for 2 hours.

Before serving, whip the cream and icing sugar into soft peaks in a large bowl. Thinly slice 1 lime. Spoon the cream over the top of the tart and arrange the lime slices on top. Finish with a grating of lime zest then cut into squares and serve.

BERRY, FIG & APPLE

★

CUSTARD SLICES

These little pastries are so easy to make and can be served for breakfast, brunch or tea. Try different fruit combinations, and add a little spoonful of jam each if you fancy.

 SERVES 6

 TAKES 35 minutes

320-g (11-oz) pack pre-rolled puff pastry

1 medium dessert apple

1 lemon

2 small figs

100g (3½oz) mixed berries, such as strawberries, blueberries and raspberries

1 tsp cornflour (cornstarch)

1 tsp icing (confectioners') sugar, plus extra for dusting

120ml (4fl oz) ready-made vanilla custard

2 tbsp ground almonds

1 egg, beaten

Preheat the oven to 200°C/400°F/gas mark 6.

Unroll the pastry sheet onto a baking sheet lined with greaseproof paper. Cut the pastry into six 12-cm (5-in) squares. Score a rough 2-cm (¾-in) border around the edge of each square.

Thinly slice the apple into rounds, drizzle with a little lemon juice and toss together in a bowl. Thinly slice the figs and add to the bowl.

Place the berries in another small bowl and toss with the cornflour and icing sugar.

Mix the vanilla custard with the ground almonds in a bowl. Divide this mixture between the pastries and spread over the centre of each in a thin even layer. Arrange the apple slices and berries on top and sprinkle with a little more icing sugar. Brush the egg over the pastry border and place the slices in the oven for 15–20 minutes until golden and risen. Serve immediately with another dusting of icing sugar.

CLASSIC

★

TARTE TATIN

Another French classic dessert that can be whipped up
easily and delivers a big wow to the table! You can vary
the flavours by using plums, pears, bananas or pineapple
instead of the traditional apple.

SERVES 6–8

TAKES 55 minutes

100g (3½oz) golden caster
(superfine) sugar
2 tbsp brandy or calvados
1 tsp vanilla bean paste
4 medium dessert apples, peeled,
cored and quartered
50g (1¾oz) salted butter, cut into
cubes
33-cm (13-in) round of ready-
rolled puff pastry
2 tbsp blanched, toasted
hazelnuts, roughly chopped
prune vinegar and hazelnut or
vanilla ice cream, to serve
(optional)

Preheat the oven to 200°C/400°F/gas mark 6.

Take a 24-cm (9½-in) ovenproof, heavy-bottom
frying pan and add the golden caster sugar, brandy
and vanilla bean paste. Place over a medium heat
and swirl the pan around to help the sugar dissolve.
Once it has dissolved, allow the mix to bubble
until it turns a light brown caramel (this will take
5–10 minutes.

Arrange the apple quarters in the pan, cut side up,
and reduce the heat to low. Cook for a further
5 minutes.

Dot over the butter and turn off the heat. Quickly
place the puff pastry round over the top of the pan
and roll up the edges to make a crust. Cut a small
slit in the centre of the pastry to allow the steam
to escape.

Place the pan in the oven and bake for 25 minutes.
Once baked allow to sit for 2 minutes then
carefully and confidently flip the tart out onto
a serving plate or board. Serve with a scattering
of hazelnuts, and prune vinegar or ice cream, if
you like.

DESSERT

★

TARTS

HONG KONG

★

EGG TARTS WITH GINGER

A staple of every good bakery in Hong Kong, this is a speedier version of the traditional recipe. I've added a little ginger syrup and chopped stem ginger to the mix and top, both of which add a touch of heat.

 MAKES 24

 TAKES 1 hour

500-g (1lb 2-oz) pack shortcrust pastry
2 tbsp icing (confectioners') sugar
6 pieces of jarred stem ginger in syrup, 3 finely chopped and 3 halved and thinly sliced for decoration
50g (1¾oz) golden caster (superfine) sugar
3 tbsp ginger syrup (from the jar of stem ginger)
2 eggs
75ml (2½fl oz) evaporated milk
1 tsp vanilla extract
1 tsp cornflour (cornstarch)

Roll out the pastry between 2 sheets of greaseproof paper to 3mm (⅛in) thick, sprinkling the icing sugar over the pastry as you roll. Use a 7-cm (3-in) fluted cutter to stamp out 24 rounds and use these to line two 12-hole shallow tart tins. Sprinkle a pinch of stem ginger into each tart case. Chill in the fridge while you make the custard. Preheat the oven to 200°C/400°F/gas mark 6.

Place the sugar in a heatproof bowl and pour over 100ml (3½fl oz) boiling water. Stir until the sugar has dissolved, then add the ginger syrup.

In a separate bowl whisk together the eggs, evaporated milk, vanilla extract and cornflour. Add 3 tbsp sugar syrup, one at a time, whisking well, then slowly add the rest and stir again. Strain the mixture through a sieve into a jug. Divide the custard between the pastry cases and bake them for 10 minutes. Reduce the oven temperature to 160°C/320°F/gas mark 3 and bake for a further 5–8 minutes until set.

Skirt a knife around each tart to release them from any baked-on custard. Allow to cool in the tin for a few minutes, then transfer to a wire rack. Top each with 2 slivers of ginger and serve warm or cold.

CANADIAN
★
BUTTER TARTS

Comforting, buttery and perfect for an autumnal afternoon with coffee after a long walk. There's even an annual festival held in Ontario dedicated to these tarts, where enthusiasts can sample all sorts of flavour combinations.

 MAKES 8 TARTS

 TAKES 1 hour, plus chilling

3 tbsp raisins
60ml (2fl oz) brandy (or apple juice)
300g (10½oz) plain (all-purpose) flour
a pinch of table salt
200g (7oz) cold, unsalted butter, cut into cubes, plus a little extra for greasing
2 tbsp desiccated coconut
1 egg yolk, plus 2 eggs
125g (4½oz) soft light brown sugar
100ml (3½fl oz) maple syrup
1 tsp cider vinegar
1 tsp vanilla extract

Place the raisins and brandy in a small bowl to soak.

Rub together the flour, salt and 150g (5oz) butter in a bowl, then stir in the coconut. Add the egg yolk and 2 tbsp ice-cold water and bring everything together with your hands. Wrap in clingfilm (plastic wrap) and chill in the fridge for 1 hour.

Melt the remaining butter in a saucepan over a low heat. Place the sugar in a mixing bowl then pour in the butter, mixing to form a paste. Add the maple syrup, eggs, cider vinegar and vanilla extract and stir.

Roll out the pastry to 3mm (⅛in) thick. Cut out eight 12-cm (5-in) circles and use to line eight 10-cm (4-in) loose-bottom tart tins, allowing overhang. You may have to re-roll the pastry to line 8 cases. Prick the bases and chill in the fridge for 30 minutes. Preheat the oven to 180°C/350°F/gas mark 4.

Blind bake the cases for 10 minutes. Remove the greaseproof paper and baking beans and bake for a further 5 minutes. Allow to cool slightly before trimming the edges. Drain the raisins and sprinkle a few into each case. Spoon the custard on top and bake for 15–20 minutes. Allow to cool slightly, then remove from the tins and transfer to a wire rack.

TREACLE

TART

This recipe reflects the Brits' love of puddings and sugar, and their skill in creating something delicious from simple ingredients. A small slice of this is all you need, served with hot custard or cream.

SERVES 12

TAKES 1 hour 5 minutes, plus chilling

230g (8oz) plain (all-purpose) flour
a pinch of table salt
115g (4oz) unsalted, cold butter cut into cubes (or a mix of half butter and half lard)
1 egg yolk
400g (14oz) golden syrup
90g (3oz) fresh breadcrumbs
½ tsp ground ginger
finely grated zest and juice of 1 lemon

Rub the flour, salt and butter together in a mixing bowl. Make a well in the centre and add the egg yolk and 2 tbsp ice-cold water. Use a dinner knife to mix, then use your hands to bring everything together to form a rough dough. Wrap in clingfilm (plastic wrap) and chill in the fridge for 1 hour.

Place a 23-cm (9-in) pastry ring on a baking sheet lined with greaseproof paper. Roll out the pastry to 3mm (⅛in) thick and use to line the pastry case, trimming any excess. Prick the base all over and chill in the fridge for 30 minutes.

Preheat the oven to 180°C/350°F/gas mark 4.

Blind bake the pastry case for 10 minutes, then remove the greaseproof paper and baking beans and bake for a further 10 minutes until golden.

Meanwhile, mix the golden syrup, breadcrumbs, ginger, lemon zest and 2 tbsp lemon juice in a bowl.

Pour the syrup mixture into the pastry case and bake for 25 minutes until just set. Serve warm or cold with custard or cream.

TORTA DELLA

★

NONNA

Torta della nonna translates from Italian to English as Grandmother's cake. Sometimes made with ricotta this version is filled with a lemony custard, which is also traditional.

 SERVES 8–10

TAKES 1 hour 30 minutes, plus chilling and cooling

230g (8oz) plain (all-purpose) flour
½ tsp baking powder
a pinch of table salt
100g (3½oz) chilled, unsalted butter, cut into cubes
150g (5oz) caster (superfine) sugar
finely grated zest of 1 lemon
1 egg yolk, plus 2 eggs
350ml (12fl oz) whole milk, plus a little for brushing
3 strips of lemon peel
1 tsp vanilla bean paste
2 tbsp pine nuts
icing (confectioners') sugar, for dusting

To make the pastry, place 200g (7oz) of the flour, baking powder and salt in a mixing bowl and mix together. Rub the butter into the flour then stir in 50g (1¾oz) of the sugar and the lemon zest. Make a well in the centre and stir in the egg yolk with 2 tbsp ice-cold water using a dinner knife, then use your hands to bring everything together to form a rough dough. Pat the pastry into a disc, wrap in clingfilm (plastic wrap) and chill in the fridge for 1 hour.

Meanwhile, place the milk in a medium saucepan over a low heat with the lemon peel and allow to slowly steam for about 5 minutes (do not boil). Crack the 2 whole eggs into a large heatproof mixing bowl and whisk in the remaining 30g (2 tbsp) of flour, 100g (3½oz) caster sugar and the vanilla bean paste. Allow the milk to sit for a couple of minutes with the heat off. Remove the lemon peel and gradually pour the milk into the mixing bowl, whisking all the time. Quickly clean out the pan, pour in the mixture and return to a low heat.

method continued overleaf...

★ ★

SOUTH AFRICAN SPICED MELKTART
continued...

Place over a low heat, stirring continuously for about 10 minutes, until the custard is thickened and coats the back of a spoon. Turn off the heat and leave to cool.

Once the pastry has chilled, remove it from the fridge and roll out to 3mm (⅛in) thick. Use it to line a 23-cm (9-in) loose-bottom tart tin then place the tin on a baking sheet. Prick the base with a fork and chill in the fridge for 30 minutes.

Preheat the oven to 180°C/350°F/gas mark 4.

When the pastry has chilled, remove it from the fridge and blind bake for 15 minutes. Remove from oven, take out the greaseproof paper and baking beans and bake for a further 10 minutes until cooked through.

Pour the filling into the tart case and return to the oven for 20 minutes until set. Once the tart is baked remove it from the oven and allow to cool for a few minutes, then carefully remove it from the tin and transfer to a wire rack to cool completely.

Take a stencil (if you have one) and dust over the ground cinnamon and icing sugar. Serve cold.

GREEK

⭐

CUSTARD TART

A take on the Greek dessert *galaktoboureko*, this is a simple filo tart packed full of fragrant herby flavours.

  SERVES 10

 TAKES 1 hour 15 minutes

70g (2½oz) unsalted butter, melted
four 40 x 30-cm (16 x 12-in) filo
  pastry sheets
2 tbsp dried breadcrumbs
3 tbsp walnuts, finely crushed,
  plus a few to decorate
500ml (17½fl oz) whole milk
2 bay leaves
2 sprigs of lemon thyme, plus a
  few extra sprigs to decorate
2 eggs, plus 1 egg yolk
50g (1¾oz) golden caster
  (superfine) sugar
75g (2½ oz) fine semolina
1 tsp vanilla extract
1 tbsp thyme honey (or use
  normal runny honey)

Preheat the oven to 180°C/350°F/gas mark 4. Grease a 20-cm (8-in) loose-bottom cake tin with melted butter. Lay one filo sheet in the tin and scatter over a thin layer of breadcrumbs and walnuts. Repeat with the remaining filo sheets, laying them at an angle each time. Roughly roll up a crust and brush with more butter. Blind bake for 10 minutes then remove the paper and baking beans and bake for a further 5 minutes. Remove from the oven.

Place the milk, bay and lemon thyme in a saucepan. Bring to a simmer then take off the heat and allow the herbs to infuse the milk for 5 minutes.

In a bowl whisk the eggs, egg yolk and sugar. Stir in the semolina. Remove the herbs from the milk and slowly whisk it into the semolina mix. Clean out the milk pan and then pour the custard back in. Stir continuously over a low heat for 5 minutes until the custard coats the back of spoon.

Remove from the heat and stir in 2 tbsp melted butter and the vanilla. Pour the mixture into the pastry case and bake for 10 minutes. Reduce the heat to 160°C/320°F/gas mark 3. Bake for a further 20 minutes until set. Serve warm with a drizzle of honey and a few walnut pieces scattered over.

MAPLE

PECAN PIE

This version of the classic pecan pie includes a more biscuity pastry and bourbon whiskey, and can be served warm or cold. It's best with some vanilla ice cream or clotted cream dolloped on top.

SERVES 8

TAKES 1 hour 15 minutes, plus chilling

250g (9oz) plain (all-purpose) flour
2 tbsp caster (superfine) sugar
a pinch of table salt
150g (5oz) cold unsalted butter, cut into cubes, plus 2 tbsp melted butter
finely grated zest of 1 orange
1 tsp vanilla bean paste
1 egg yolk
200g (7oz) pecan nuts, roughly chopped, plus 50g whole pecans to decorate
3 eggs
40g (1½ oz) soft light brown sugar
80g (2¾ oz) maple syrup
1 tsp vanilla extract
2 tbsp bourbon whiskey

Rub together the flour, caster sugar, salt and butter in a large mixing bowl. Stir in the orange zest and vanilla bean paste and make a well in the centre. Add the egg yolk and 2 tbsp ice-cold water. Use a dinner knife to mix everything then use your hands to bring together a rough dough. Wrap in clingfilm (plastic wrap) and chill in the fridge for 1 hour.

Place a 23-cm (9-in) pastry ring on a baking sheet lined with greaseproof paper. Roll out the pastry to 3mm (⅛in) thick. Use this to line the pastry case, trimming any excess, and prick the base all over. Chill in the fridge for 30 minutes. Preheat the oven to 180°C/350°F/gas mark 4.

Blind bake the tart case for 10 minutes then remove the greaseproof paper and baking beans and bake for a further 10 minutes until lightly golden. Allow to cool a little, then trim the edges.

Place the chopped pecans, eggs, soft light brown sugar, maple syrup, vanilla extract and whiskey in a bowl and mix well. Spoon into the tart case and arrange the whole pecans over the top. Bake the tart for 35 minutes until set. Allow to cool slightly, then carefully remove the tart from the tin and transfer to a wire rack to cool completely.

CHOCOLATE
★
PEAR TART

A fantastic flavour combination, chocolate and pears make for a decadent dessert. You can grind your own nuts by blitzing blanched hazelnuts in a food processor.

SERVES 10

TAKES 1 hour 55 minutes, plus chilling

250g (9oz) plain (all-purpose) flour
2 tbsp ground almonds
2 tbsp cocoa powder
2 tbsp icing (confectioners') sugar
a pinch of table salt
125g (4½oz) cold unsalted butter,
    cut into cubes, plus 180g (6¼oz)
    unsalted butter, softened
3 yolks, plus 2 eggs
1 tbsp almond or hazelnut liquor
    (optional)
200g (7oz) dark chocolate
    (minimum 70% cocoa solids)
180g (6¼oz) golden caster
    (superfine) sugar, plus extra for
    sprinkling
150g (5oz) ground hazelnuts or
    ground almonds
2 pears, peeled, cored and cut into
    quarters

Place the 175g (6oz) of the flour, the ground almonds, cocoa powder, icing sugar and salt in a large mixing bowl and stir together. Add the 125g (4½oz) cold unsalted butter and rub it into the flour. Make a well in the centre, add 1 egg yolk and 2 tbsp ice-cold water. Use a dinner knife to mix everything in then use your hands to bring it together into a rough dough. Pat the pastry into a disc, cover in clingfilm (plastic wrap) and chill in the fridge for 30 minutes.

Once the pastry has chilled, remove from the fridge, roll out to 3mm (⅛in) thick and use it to line a 23-cm (9-in) deep loose-bottom tart tin. Prick the base all over with a fork and place back in the fridge for 1 hour.

Preheat the oven to 180°C/350°F/gas mark 4.

Remove the tart case from the fridge and place on baking sheet. Blind bake in the oven for 10 minutes, then remove the greaseproof paper and baking beans and return to the oven for a further 5–10 minutes until the pastry is cooked through.

method continued overleaf...

CHOCOLATE PEAR TART
continued...

Meanwhile, make the filling. Melt 150g (5oz) of the chocolate in a heatproof bowl over a saucepan of barely simmering water. Roughly chop the remaining chocolate and place to one side.

Reduce the oven temperature to 160°C/320°F/ gas mark 3.

In a large mixing bowl beat together the 180g (6¼oz) softened butter and golden caster sugar until pale and fluffy. Beat in the 2 eggs and 2 yolks one at a time along with the liquor, if using. Pour in the melted chocolate, ground nuts and remaining 75g (2½oz) flour and use a large metal spoon to gently fold everything together. Pour the mixture into the pastry case and arrange the pears on top. Sprinkle over a little golden caster sugar.

Place the tart in the oven and bake for 1 hour 10 minutes until just set. Remove from the oven and allow to cool for a few minutes in the tin, then carefully remove the tart from the tin and transfer to a wire rack to cool completely. Serve with crème fraîche.

GRAPEFRUIT & CAMPARI
★
MERINGUE PIES

These little tartlets take a little bit of work but they look so special. Adding Campari to the grapefruit curd is optional, but this herby, citrussy aperitif gives a slightly bitter note that works beautifully with the sweet meringue.

MAKES 16

TAKES 1 hour 30 minutes, plus cooling

250g (9oz) plain (all-purpose) flour
a pinch of table salt
3 tbsp icing (confectioners') sugar
175g (6oz) cold unsalted butter, cut into cubes, plus a little melted butter for greasing
1 tsp vanilla bean paste
finely grated zest and juice of 3 pink grapefruits
finely grated zest and juice of 1 lemon
2 eggs, plus 3 egg yolks and 4 egg whites
475g (1lb 1oz) caster (superfine) sugar
3 tbsp cornflour (cornstarch)
2 tbsp Campari (optional)

In a bowl rub 125g (4½oz) of the butter into the flour, salt and icing sugar. Make a well in the centre and add 1 egg yolk, 2 tbsp ice-cold water and the vanilla paste. Mix with a dinner knife then bring together with your hands to form a dough. Wrap in clingfilm (plastic wrap) and chill in the fridge for 1 hour.

Whisk together the fruit juices and zests, whole eggs, remaining egg yolks, 250g (9oz) caster sugar and cornflour in a saucepan. Add the Campari, if using, and remaining 50g (1¾oz) butter then stir over a low-medium heat for 5–10 minutes until the mixture coats the back of a spoon. Pass through a sieve, transfer to a clean bowl, cover with clingfilm (plastic wrap) and place to one side to cool.

Take a two 12-hole fluted tart tins and lightly grease each hole with melted butter. Once the pastry has chilled, cut it in half and roll out each piece to 3mm (⅛in) thick. Using a pastry cutter or small plate for guidance, cut out eight 8-cm (3-in) circles and line each hole. Prick the bases all over with a fork and chill in the fridge for 30 minutes.

method continued overleaf...

★ ★ ★ ★ ★ ★ ★ ★ ★ ★ ★ ★ ★ ★ ★ ★ ★

GRAPEFRUIT & CAMPARI MERINGUE PIES
continued...

Preheat the oven to 180°C/350°F/gas mark 4.

Blind bake the pastry for 10 minutes. Remove the greaseproof paper and baking beans and bake for a further 5–10 minutes until golden and baked through. Remove the tin from the oven and allow to cool for a few minutes then carefully remove the individual cases from the tin and transfer to a wire rack to cool completely.

Place the egg whites in a large, clean mixing bowl and whisk with an electric hand whisk to stiff peaks, then place to one side.

Place the remaining 225g (8oz) caster sugar with 6 tbsp water in a medium saucepan and heat to 120°C/248°F (use a sugar thermometer). When the temperature is reached pour the syrup as a slow, steady stream into the bowl of egg whites, whisking continuously. Whisk until the meringue is cool (about 15 minutes).

Place the tart cases on a serving board and spoon in the grapefruit curd. Spoon the meringue on top and use the back of a spoon to form a peak. Use a blowtorch to colour the meringue or place the tarts on a tray under the grill.

SWEET PLUM

★

'BRIOCHE'

Inspired by the core ingredients of German plum cakes
known as *pflaumenkuchen* or *zwetschgenkuchen* this is a great
tea time treat hot out of the oven. Crumble over the streusel
topping from page 121 just before baking, if you like.

MAKES 2 TARTS

TAKES 40 minutes, plus
proving

450g (1lb) strong white bread flour,
plus extra for dusting
50g (1¾oz) wholemeal
(wholewheat) bread flour
50g (1¾oz) ground almonds
a pinch of table salt
240ml (8fl oz) whole milk
½ x 7g (¼oz) sachet dried fast-
action yeast
1 tsp golden caster (superfine)
sugar
1 egg yolk
melted unsalted butter, for
greasing
400g (14oz) ripe plums, halved,
de-stoned and sliced
2 tbsp demerara sugar
2 tsp coarse polenta
4 tbsp blueberry jam (jelly)
100g (3½oz) marzipan
2 tbsp uncooked streusel mix
(optional, see page 121)
2 tbsp toasted flaked almonds

Mix the flours, ground almonds and salt in a large
bowl and make a well in the centre. Gently warm
the milk in a saucepan until lukewarm then stir
in the yeast and golden caster sugar until frothy.
Stir the milk into the flour, add the egg yolk and
butter then use your hands to bring the dough
together. Tip out onto a lightly floured work
surface and knead for a few minutes. Grease a large
clean bowl with butter and add the dough. Cover
with clingfilm (plastic wrap) and put in warm place
for 1 hour until doubled in size.

Meanwhile, in a bowl toss the plums with the
demerara sugar.

Preheat the oven to 200°C/400°F/gas mark 6.

Knock back the dough and turn it out onto a
lightly floured work surface. Halve the dough and
roll each piece into a 30-cm (12-in) round. Dust
2 baking sheets with polenta and place a round
of dough on each. Spoon the blueberry jam over
the dough circles and dot over the marzipan.
Arrange the plum slices on top and scatter over the
uncooked streusel mix, if using. Bake the tarts for
20 minutes until risen and jammy. Scatter over the
toasted flaked almonds and serve hot with cream.

FIG

★

TART

Fresh figs, sitting on top of light and creamy ricotta yogurt and a crisp shortcrust base, take centre stage in this simple dessert.

  SERVES 6

TAKES 45 minutes

33-cm (13-in) round of ready-
  rolled shortcrust pastry
1 egg, beaten
4 tbsp caster (superfine) sugar
2 tbsp water
3 tbsp unsalted pistachios,
  finely chopped
100g (3½oz) ricotta
finely grated zest of 1 orange
200g (7oz) Greek yogurt
2 tbsp fig jam (jelly)
6–8 fresh figs, quartered
1 tbsp runny honey

Preheat the oven to 180°C/350°F/gas mark 4.

Unroll the pastry round onto a baking sheet lined with greaseproof paper. Score a 3-cm (1¼-in) border around the edge and brush with beaten egg. Bake in the oven for 20–25 minutes until golden. Remove from the oven and allow to cool on a wire rack.

Place the caster sugar and water in a small saucepan and bring to the boil, then turn down the heat to low. Carefully swirl the syrup in the pan as it bubbles for 1–2 minutes; as soon as you have a golden syrup, brush it onto the pastry border and sprinkle over 2 tbsp of the pistachios.

Place the ricotta in a bowl and beat well with a wooden spoon. In a separate bowl add the orange zest to the Greek yogurt then fold in the ricotta. Place to one side.

Spread the fig jam over the base of the pastry and top with the creamy ricotta mixture. Arrange the figs over the top and drizzle over the honey. Scatter over the remaining chopped pistachios and serve straight away.

FROZEN BLACK FOREST
★
CHERRY TART

A fun dessert to bring out at special occasions, this is perfect for holiday celebrations or a summer party. It's easy to make and keep in the freezer, ready just to pull out and decorate when needed.

 SERVES 10

 TAKES 25 minutes, plus at least 8 hours chilling

1 x 440g (1lb) can cherries, drained
2 tbsp kirsch
300g (10½oz) dark chocolate digestive biscuits (graham crackers)
100g (3½oz) unsalted butter, melted
400g (14oz) chocolate ice cream
3 tbsp cherry jam (jelly)
50g (1¾oz) milk chocolate
150ml (5fl oz) double (heavy) cream
1 tbsp icing (confectioners') sugar
1 tsp vanilla bean paste
50g (1¾oz) fresh or frozen cherries

Place the canned cherries in a small saucepan with the kirsch and bring to the boil. Turn the heat down and simmer for 2 minutes, then place to one side.

Blitz the digestive biscuits in a food processor to breadcrumb consistency, then tip into a bowl and stir in the melted butter. Pack the biscuit crumbs into a 20-cm (8-in) loose-bottom tart tin then chill in the fridge for at least 2 hours.

Once the base has set take the ice cream from the freezer and allow to soften a little.

Drain the cherries and place to one side. Spoon the jam into the base of the case and scatter over the cherries and 40g (1½oz) of the milk chocolate, chopped into chocolate chip-sized pieces.

Spoon in the ice cream and smooth over. Place the tart in the freezer for at least 6 hours.

When you are ready to serve, lightly whip the cream, icing sugar and vanilla bean paste in a bowl.

Remove the tart from the tin and place on a serving plate. Pile the cream up in the middle of the tart, top with fresh or frozen cherries and grate over the remaining chocolate. Serve immediately.

TARTE AUX
★
FRAMBOISES

Fresh raspberries and vanilla pastry cream! The perfect filling for an afternoon tea pastry. You can easily use this recipe to make tartlets, which would take centre stage on any cake stand.

 SERVES 8–10

 TAKES 1 hour 10 minutes, plus chilling

500-g (1lb 2-oz) pack shortcrust pastry
2 tbsp icing (confectioners') sugar
270ml (9fl oz) whole milk
2 tsp vanilla bean paste
40g (1½oz) caster (superfine) sugar
2 tbsp cornflour (cornstarch)
3 egg yolks
120ml (4fl oz) double (heavy) cream
450g (1lb) fresh raspberries
4 tbsp seedless raspberry jam (jelly)
1 lemon

Roll out the pastry to about 3mm (⅛in) thick, sprinkling with icing sugar as you go, and use it to line a 23-cm (9-in) square fluted loose-bottom tart tin. Prick the base all over with a fork and chill in the fridge for 1 hour.

Meanwhile, place the milk and vanilla bean paste in a medium saucepan over a low heat for a few minutes until steaming. Remove from the heat and leave the milk to sit for a couple of minutes.

Place the caster sugar, cornflour and egg yolks in a large mixing bowl and whisk well. One at a time, whisk 5 tbsp warm milk into the bowl, then slowly pour the remaining milk in, whisking continuously. Quickly clean out the pan and return to the hob. Pour in the egg mixture and whisk over a low heat for about 5 minutes until it's thick enough to coat the back of a spoon. Pour the custard into a clean bowl and leave to cool with a piece of greaseproof paper on top to stop a skin forming as it cools.

Preheat the oven to 180°C/350°F/gas mark 4.

method continued overleaf...

TARTE AUX FRAMBOISES

continued...

Once the pastry case has chilled, remove it from the fridge, place on a baking sheet and blind bake for 15 minutes. Remove the greaseproof paper and baking beans and return to the oven for a further 5–10 minutes until golden and cooked through. Cool on a wire rack.

In a bowl, whisk the cream into soft peaks then gently fold through the custard. Spoon the creamy custard over the base of the cooled tart case and arrange the raspberries over the top.

Place the raspberry jam and a good squeeze of lemon juice in a small microwaveable bowl and microwave on a low heat until spreadable. Alternatively, if you don't have a microwave, heat in a small saucepan over a low heat. Add a little more lemon juice if needed. Drizzle the jam over the tart and serve immediately.

PASSION FRUIT, MANGO &
★
CHOCOLATE TART

What a combo, especially for those of us who don't know
whether we're in the chocolate or fruit dessert camp.

SERVES 8–10

TAKES 1 hour 25 minutes,
plus chilling and setting

175g (6oz) plain (all-purpose) flour
2 tbsp ground almonds
2 tbsp cocoa powder
100g (3½oz) icing (confectioners')
  sugar
a pinch of table salt
150g (5oz) cold unsalted butter,
  cut into cubes
2 egg yolks
8 passion fruits
50g (1¾oz) unsalted cashews
170g (6oz) white chocolate
200ml (7fl oz) double (heavy)
  cream
2 tbsp cornflour (cornstarch)
1 tsp vanilla bean paste
500g (1lb 2oz) ripe mango, peeled,
  de-stoned and sliced
1 tbsp caster (superfine) sugar,
  for the brûlée top

Place the flour, ground almonds, cocoa powder,
40g (1½oz) of the icing sugar and the salt in a large
mixing bowl and stir together. Add the butter and
rub it into the flour then make a well in the centre
and add the egg yolks and 2 tbsp ice-cold water.
Use a dinner knife to mix everything, then use your
hands to bring it together into a rough dough. Pat
the pastry into a disc, cover in clingfilm (plastic
wrap) and chill in the fridge for 1 hour.

Meanwhile, halve 6 of the passion fruits and scrape
out the pulp into a sieve set over a bowl. Press all
the flesh and juice through into the bowl and then
discard the seeds.

Once the pastry has chilled, roll out to 3mm (⅛in)
thick and line a 20-cm (8-in) loose-bottom tart tin,
allowing for some overhang. Prick the base of the
case all over and chill in the fridge for a further
30 minutes.

Preheat the oven to 180°C/350°F/gas mark 4.

method continued overleaf...

★ ★ ★ ★ ★ ★ ★ ★ ★ ★ ★ ★ ★ ★ ★ ★

PASSION FRUIT, MANGO & CHOCOLATE TART
continued...

Once the pastry has chilled, place the tart tin on a baking sheet and blind bake for 15 minutes. Remove the greaseproof paper and baking beans and bake for a further 5–10 minutes until crisp and cooked through. Allow to cool on a wire rack and then carefully trim the over hanging pastry with a Swiss peeler.

Meanwhile rinse the cashews in cold water and toss with 1 tbsp icing sugar in a roasting tray. Bake for 10–15 minutes until golden and place to one side.

Chop the white chocolate and place in a small saucepan with the cream, 40g (1½oz) of the icing sugar, the cornflour and vanilla bean paste. Whisk continuously and gently until melted and thickened. Remove from the heat then stir in the passion fruit pulp.

Pour the filling into the pastry case and arrange half of the mango slices on top. Chill in the fridge for at least 2 hours.

Just before you are ready to serve, place the remaining mango in a blender with 1 tbsp icing sugar. Blitz well and pass through a sieve. Halve the remaining 2 passion fruits and scoop out the seeds into a bowl.

When you're ready to serve, take the tart from the fridge. Sprinkle over the caster sugar and caramelise it with a blowtorch or under a hot grill. Scatter the roasted cashews around the edge. To serve, cut into slices and top each slice with a spoonful of passion fruit seeds and a little mango purée.

QUICK BERRY
★
WHITE CHOCOLATE TARTS

Combining seasonal summer fruit, fresh mint and a dash
of prosecco, and so quick and easy to prepare, these are
perfect for a summer party.

SERVES 6

TAKES 20 minutes

50g (1¾oz) white chocolate
1 tbsp unsalted butter
170ml (6fl oz) double (heavy)
  cream
100g (3½oz) mascarpone
finely grated zest of 1 lemon
six 10-cm (4-in) pre-baked sweet
  shortcrust pastry cases
200g (7oz) mixed berries, eg
  strawberries, raspberries
  and cherries
50ml (2fl oz) prosecco
a splash of rose water
a few sprigs of mint, leaves picked
20g (¾oz) ready-made meringue
  kisses (optional)

Place the white chocolate in a heatproof bowl over
a saucepan of barely simmering water. Melt the
chocolate then add the butter, stirring until melted.
Place to one side. Beat 70ml (2½fl oz) of the double
cream and the mascarpone together in a medium
bowl then fold in the melted chocolate and lemon
zest. Place the pastry cases on a tray and spoon the
creamy mixture into them. Place in the fridge while
you prepare the toppings.

Toss the berries together in a bowl with the
prosecco and rose water. Crush the mint leaves
lightly and add to the bowl, then toss again. Lightly
whip the remaining double cream to soft peaks.
Crush up the meringues, if using.

Take the pastry cases from the fridge. Spoon a
little whipped cream onto each. Drain the berries
and arrange these on top of the cream. Sprinkle
over the meringue, if using, and scatter over the
remaining mint leaves. Serve straight away.

ORANGE BLOSSOM, PEACH &
APRICOT FILO

The perfect pudding for a sunny summer's day! Don't be scared of the orange blossom water – it goes perfectly with the sweet apricots.

SERVES 4

TAKES 45 minutes

five 30 x 30-cm (12 x 12-in) filo pastry sheets
40g (1½oz) unsalted butter, melted
1 tbsp ground cinnamon
1 tbsp icing (confectioners') sugar, plus extra for dusting
8 dried apricots (or 4 fresh, if in season, halved and de-stoned
4 small figs, halved
2 fresh ripe peaches, halved and de-stoned
1 cinnamon stick
1 tbsp orange blossom water
2 tbsp runny honey
100g (3½oz) Greek yogurt
100g (3½oz) mascarpone

Preheat the oven to 200°C/400°F/gas mark 6.

Line a baking sheet with greaseproof paper. Lay a filo sheet on top, brush with melted butter and sprinkle with a little cinnamon and icing sugar. Repeat with the remaining sheets of filo. Fold over the edges of the filo pastry to make a border and brush with butter. Bake the filo for 15 minutes until golden brown then transfer to a wire rack to cool.

Place the fruit, cinnamon stick, orange blossom water, runny honey and 400ml (14fl oz) water in a saucepan over a medium heat and bring to a simmer. Turn the heat down and gently poach the fruit for 15–20 minutes until soft, turning the fruit every so often. Use a slotted spoon to remove the fruit from the syrup and place in a dish. Over a medium heat reduce the syrup by about two-thirds.

Mix the yogurt with the mascarpone in a small mixing bowl.

When ready to serve, top the filo with the yogurt mix and spoon over the fruit. Drizzle over the syrup and sprinkle with a light dusting of icing sugar. Slice up and serve immediately.

NO-BAKE OREO

★

CHOCOLATE PEANUT TART

This is so easy to make but super-rich – a sliver is more
than enough – so you'll get a lot of servings from this tart.
No baking is required, just a few hours of chilling so it's
a great one to make in advance for a dinner party.

SERVES 16

TAKES 30 minutes, plus
chilling and setting

2 x 154-g (5½-oz) packs Oreo
  cookies
75g (2½oz) salted butter, melted
2 tbsp crunchy peanut butter
300ml (10fl oz) double (heavy)
  cream
1 tsp cornflour (cornstarch)
250g (9oz) dark chocolate, finely
  chopped
50g (1¾oz) unsalted butter,
  softened
2 tbsp whole milk
a pinch of sea salt
150g (5oz) roasted unsalted
  peanuts, finely chopped
4 tbsp ready-made thick caramel
  sauce (optional)
cocoa powder, to serve

Place the Oreo cookies in a food processor and
blitz to crumbs. Tip the crumbs into a large mixing
bowl, stir in the melted butter and peanut butter
and mix well. Spoon the biscuit mix into a 23-cm
(9-in) deep, fluted tart tin and press it into the base
and up the sides. Chill the tin in the fridge for at
least 1 hour.

Meanwhile, mix 1 tbsp double cream with the
cornflour in a bowl. Place the remaining double
cream in a medium saucepan over a low heat. Once
the cream is gently steaming, remove from the
heat and whisk in the chocolate, cornflour paste
and unsalted butter. Whisk until smooth, stir in the
milk and sprinkle in the sea salt, then allow to cool
for about 20 minutes. Take the tart case from the
fridge and scatter the chopped peanuts over the
base. Spoon over the caramel sauce, if using. Pour
the chocolate sauce over the nuts and caramel
then smooth over. Place the tart in the fridge to
chill and set for about 2 hours before serving. Dust
with cocoa powder and serve in thin wedges with
a cup of coffee. This tart will last for about 2 days
in the fridge.

INDEX

★★

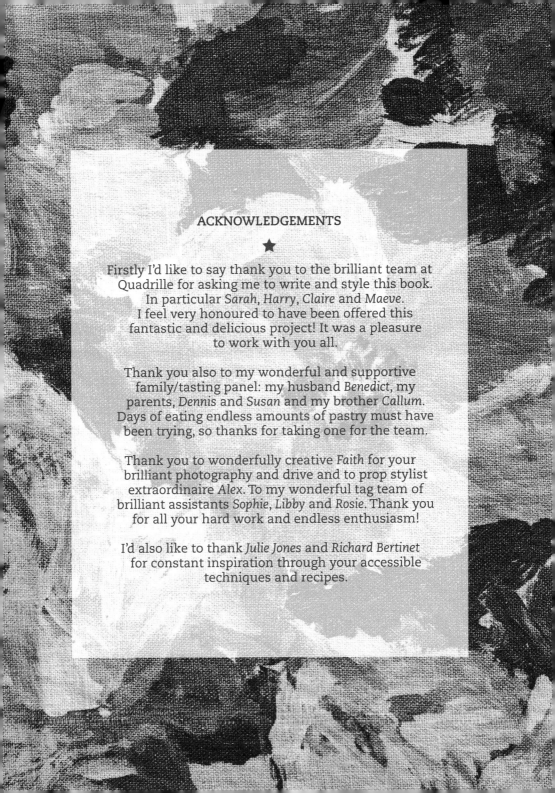

ACKNOWLEDGEMENTS

★

Firstly I'd like to say thank you to the brilliant team at Quadrille for asking me to write and style this book. In particular *Sarah*, *Harry*, *Claire* and *Maeve*. I feel very honoured to have been offered this fantastic and delicious project! It was a pleasure to work with you all.

Thank you also to my wonderful and supportive family/tasting panel: my husband *Benedict*, my parents, *Dennis* and *Susan* and my brother *Callum*. Days of eating endless amounts of pastry must have been trying, so thanks for taking one for the team.

Thank you to wonderfully creative *Faith* for your brilliant photography and drive and to prop stylist extraordinaire *Alex*. To my wonderful tag team of brilliant assistants *Sophie*, *Libby* and *Rosie*. Thank you for all your hard work and endless enthusiasm!

I'd also like to thank *Julie Jones* and *Richard Bertinet* for constant inspiration through your accessible techniques and recipes.